The Holy Grail of Managing a Nonprofit

The Holy Grail of Managing a Nonprofit

Mark Mullen

Haddon Township, New Jersey

Library of Congress Control Number: 2017915160

Publisher's Cataloging-In-Publication Data

Names: Mullen, Mark, 1954-

Title: The holy grail of managing a nonprofit / Mark Mullen.

Description: Haddon Township, New Jersey: Mark Mullen, [2017] | Includes bibliographical references.

Identifiers: ISBN 9780999386606 (paperback) | ISBN 0999386603 (paperback) | ISBN 9780999386613 (ebook)

Subjects: LCSH: Nonprofit organizations--Management. | Nonprofit organizations--Planning. | Leadership. | Business planning. | Executive succession.

Classification: LCC HD62.6 .M85 2017 (print) | LCC HD62.6 (ebook) | DDC 658.048--dc23

Contents

FIGURES, TABLES, AND EXHIBITS

FIGURES

TABLES

EXHIBITS

Evidence on Which This Book Is Based

This book is built on a broad body of research on management and leadership in the workplace. The Holy Grail of Managing a Nonprofit is the result of countless years of studying the results of successful management strategies implemented in the world's leading for-profit and not-for- profit sectors. Case studies and the resulting outcomes learned through these field studies were also examined in detail.

Complimenting these tested and proven management initiatives is the author's twenty-five years of experience as a senior strategic leader in the public sector. As an experienced senior executive, I understand the frustrations and challenges that come from leading a public sector organization. It is not easy answering to the many stakeholders associated with a nonprofit. Leaders have responsibilities to the clients of the nonprofit's services, to the staff who create the product, to the board which governs, and to the donors and partners who support the organization. I understand these pressures and set out to write a book sharing what I have learned from my experiences and the practices of successful organizations. Rather than just telling you what I have learned, I designed this book to serve as a prototype showing you how to evaluate, analyze, and frame your data, programs, and services against your vision, mission, and budget. My goal for writing this book is to make you a better leader, employee, and caretaker of your nonprofit organization.

Finally, sometimes nonprofit organizations are apprehensive of utilizing successful business tactics. They may believe the nonprofit is too small or too different to take advantage of proven business practices. A quick reminder that the nonprofit is a business. It consumes resources to provide a product, usually in the form of services. That is the definition of business. While not all strategies presented in this book will be applicable to all nonprofits, you will find that most of the strategies can be scaled to even the smallest of nonprofit organizations. People, processes, and procedures behave similarly regardless of the size of the organization

What's In This Book?

This book contains two sections. Section one is all about leadership and its need at all levels. The success or failure of every nonprofit depends on the quality and composition of the board. A nonprofit cannot be excellent without selecting and training the right board directors. In Chapter 1, discussion on the composition of the board will guide you in the development of a healthy board. You will also be guided through board director and CEO roles and responsibilities, and succession planning. Chapter 2 prepares the CEO for managing the board through committees and meetings. An example of a dashboard showing key indicators of organizational success is provided as a way to keep the board updated all year long.

Chapter 3 will show you how to engage all employees in leadership development allowing them to make good decisions that will carry the organization into the desired future. All employees will learn to collect and use relevant and real data; to monitor the data to stay on track; to fully understand why the organization exists; how the organization conducts its business; how decisions are made; and how employee work contributes to revenue generation and organizational expenses. Engaging all employees in the business side of the nonprofit will create deeper feelings of ownership and commitment on the part of the employees. Engagement will also contribute to the making of a healthy and productive culture – one where employees think and act like a united winning organization.

Section two is all about strategic planning. In Chapter 4 you will be guided through the process of planning for the desired future. You will learn how to frame your current situation by examining and describing your business operations model. You will question and evaluate your presumed operations and mission strategies and learn how to engage the nonprofit's stakeholders in the planning process. Examining your competition and other organizations with similar missions will help you solve mission delivery challenges.

The next couple of chapters provide you with the design principles needed to create excellence. Chapter 5 will guide you through the process of framing your desired future identity by challenging you to prioritize and choose essential mission elements to be delivered in the future.

Chapter 6 will assist you with the setting of goals and objectives that will shape the boundaries – the lines in which you will paint.

In Chapter 7 you will create a strategic budget that allocates resources to priority mission activities. Budgeting requires input from all employees as they are the ones that produce both revenue and expenses. This chapter will guide you through a process for involving all staff with the assessing of individual program revenues and expenses, and making choices based on the assessments and organization's vision and strategy for the future.

Attracting and maintaining donors is all about the telling of compelling stories of individuals who have been helped by the nonprofit. Chapter 8 will suggest strategies that will enable your nonprofit to attract and maintain the donors needed to complete the creation.

When you have completed the strategic processes described in this book you will have uncovered things you did not know - and maybe didn't want to know – about the organization and its people. You will have discovered everything you need to know about the nonprofit and how to move it forward in a positive and efficient manner.

Preface

What is the difference between an average, good, and excellent nonprofit? The answer is simple. Excellent nonprofits constantly look forward. They understand that tomorrow will look, feel, and be different than yesterday. Excellent nonprofits are not victims of an undiscovered tomorrow - they create the future they want to see.

Creating a vivid future requires a well-trained and engaged employee who is empowered to challenge the status quo. Excellent nonprofits work as one body to collect, analyze, and make decisions based on relevant and real data. *The Holy Grail of Managing a Nonprofit* will show leaders how to engage all stakeholders with the collection of valuable information and how to use that data to make future-oriented decisions. You will make decisions today that will lead you to the tomorrow you want.

The Holy Grail of Managing a Nonprofit provides leaders with the tools necessary for creating real solutions for the real problems that keep you awake at night – those most important life and death issues. Use this easy-to-read book format as a blueprint for discovering your nonprofit excellence.

What should you hope to get from this book? The answer is:

- A framework and context to help you create the nonprofit of your dreams including board development and employee leadership
- Group problem solving exercises and challenges
- Helpful templates

- Sample charts
- The knowledge needed to drive the nonprofit into a desired future through strategic planning
- All employee engagement and buy-in with moving the nonprofit forward and a healthy culture
- Reassurance that change does not need to be painful

Introduction

The nonprofit industry controls more than $3 trillion in assets, and yet the industry is in danger of going the way of the large box-store retailer like Sears and J.C. Penney. The near extinction of the big box store has been caused mostly by self-inflicted wounds. Executives and board directors became complacent, assuming the world and consumers would not change. But they did change. New disruptive strategies and technologies offered by upstart companies provide customers with better purchasing experiences. The big box stores failed to notice and failed to change their strategy as repeat customers began to dwindle.

The nonprofit industry is now facing the same challenges as the retail industry. There is increased competition for monies once reserved for nonprofits. Corporate social responsibility programs, online go-fund-me initiatives, and new private foundations all provide competition for services and funding once reserved for public charities. Even once robust membership organizations are challenged as Baby Boomers retire from membership and Millennials decline professional memberships in favor of free networking and resources offered through the Internet, LinkedIn, and Facebook.

The nonprofit industry has been exceedingly slow in recognizing the old way of conducting business is over. The industries failure to act has placed additional stresses on the nonprofit. Major studies show:

- An increasing number of unprepared and under prepared CEOs at the helm of nonprofit organizations,
- Insecure boards who don't know whether to rubber-stamp or micro-manage CEO decisions,
- Loss of public trust as organizational mission, vision, and impact are poorly communicated to outside world.

In order to survive nonprofits must adopt business like practices and procedures. The nonprofit must learn to compete for resources (including employees) rather than waiting for resources to find the nonprofit. Measuring program performance and outcomes, revenue creation in a digital age, long-term investment oversight, developing new and innovative programs, and annual CEO evaluations must become standard vocabulary for nonprofit leaders.

Two things remain certain. Nonprofits must change, or they will disappear. And that change must start with strong leadership and strategy that focuses on long-term stability. Having a great mission is not enough to build and maintain a sustainable organization.

Section I: Leadership

CHAPTER ONE

Governance-Managing the Process

The nonprofit organization depends on capable, proficient, and talented individuals to fulfill their mission. Leadership comes in the form of the CEO, staff, volunteers, and the board of directors. All are important, but without effective governance provided by the board, the nonprofit will be doomed to failure.

Because the board of directors is the legal and responsible guardians of the nonprofit they must be populated with diverse, engaged, and skilled (preferably in at least one area of business, or with general business experience) individuals. This is important because the nonprofit board has two primary functions. Both are business related. They are:

1. Strategy development (value creation) and,
2. Hiring a qualified executive to manage the day-to-day operations of the nonprofit.

Within this scope the board creates policies that: (1) are vital to the future of the organization; (2) outline procedures to evaluate the executive's performance; (3) plan for the next executive should the current executive leave unexpectedly; (4) defines the role of the executive; (5) participates in and approves the strategic plan; (6) participates in and approves the annual budget and all financial plans; and (7) participates in building a healthy environment for staff and clients.

It cannot be overstated that a nonprofit's success depends on the quality of its board. A 2014 Stanford Graduate School of Business survey on nonprofit governance bears this point out[1]. The study uncovered a number of governance challenges which limit nonprofit success. Among the ones you can control are:

- Over twenty-five percent of nonprofit board directors do not have acute and comprehensive knowledge of the nonprofit's mission and strategy.
- Over thirty percent of nonprofit board directors were discouraged with their board's level of competence in evaluating organizational performance.
- A majority of nonprofit board directors did not believe their colleague board directors had the right experiences to help the nonprofit.
- Ninety-two percent of nonprofit board directors cited a lack of confidence in the quality of data used to evaluate the nonprofit's performance.

The board of directors for a nonprofit exists for one purpose, and one purpose only: to ensure that the nonprofit delivers an impactful service or benefit to the client or client community (value creation). Unfortunately, some directors erroneously believe the board exists to provide them with:

- A stepping stone to further their professional career,
- A capstone to end professional career,
- An opportunity to manage,
- An opportunity for future employment with the nonprofit.

---

[1] David F. Larcker, Nicholas E. Donatiello, Bill Meehan, Brian Tayan. 2015 Survey on Board of Directors of Nonprofit Organizations.Standford GSB. April 2015

It does not exist for any of those reasons. In the event that a board has directors like this, the CEO and board chair must take steps to re-educate and train them of the responsibilities of the board or call for their removal from the board as soon as possible. Opportunist board directors are a sign that the nonprofit needs to re-evaluate and modify its board development program.

In addition to the already mentioned responsibilities, board directors have three legal duties. They are:

1. The Duty of Care – be informed and engaged in decision-making. Showing up for the board meeting is not sufficient. Directors must study the organization and participate in discussions and decision-making.
2. The Duty of Loyalty – putting the organization's needs above professional interests. Self-interests need to be left at home.
3. The Duty of Obedience – ensure that organization follows all local, state, and federal laws. This can be accomplished through an annual checklist completed by the CEO.

Managing the Board

In order to address the challenges identified in the Stanford Study, the CEO will want to work closely with the board chair and insist on annual training for the board on each of the following topics:

- Mission & vision - how the nonprofit is currently delivering services to meet both. Project managers or program directors should assist the CEO presenting a comprehensive overview of performance on each program.

- Annual budget – how the budget is developed, how it attaches resources to services and programs. The CFO should assist the CEO and Chair with this presentation.
- Data – how and what is collected and how it relates to measuring mission, strategic outcomes, and impact.
- Working as a team – use board training expert to lead the board in trust building
- Bylaws, essential, and mandated policies reviewed annually.
- Work closely with the board chair – he/she plays a central role in establishing an environment where discussion and disagreement can occur without hostility and mistrust.

Many organizations that specialize in nonprofit management have recorded webinars on a variety of topics which can be used for board training purposes. Use them. In addition to annual training, be sure to set aside time at each board meeting for board training. This needs to be an agenda item and should occur at the beginning of the meeting when the board is rested and unhurried by time constraints.

Use Board Committees

The work of a board is best accomplished through committees. Committees composed of only a few directors can focus all of their energies on addressing particular topics – subjects that could be unwieldy and frustrating for an entire board to work through. An added bonus for the CEO is the opportunity to build positive working relationships with a handful of directors at a time. Working on committees will also give the CEO a firsthand account of what issues the board considers sacred and what issues are not so important.

Committee size will vary depending on the size of the board. Nonprofits with a large membership of directors should keep committee size in the range of five to seven. More than seven will make decision-making difficult. If the nonprofit board is small (eight to seventeen), create three person committees. Nonprofits with less than eight members should consider recruiting local business executives to serve on a committee alongside a board director and staff member.

While selecting committee participants, pair board expertise with the appropriate committee. If you don't have a particular expert on the board, consider adding a local volunteer expert to the committee. Finance, investment, and marketing expertise are three of the most common deficiencies on nonprofit boards. Be sure to get board approval on using volunteer experts before you invite on to a meeting. Some boards are leery of discussing board business in front of strangers. They shouldn't be, as transparency should be the foremost trait of board leadership.

A high functioning board should have the following committees.

1. Governance Committee (recruitment & training of board).

Recruitment efforts need to be built around the skills missing from the current board. The board must find ways to identify individuals (internal and external to the nonprofit) who possess and are willing to share those skills. One suggestion to find potential board directors is for the board to create a Governance Committee. This committee would focus on identifying, developing, and mentoring potential directors.

There are several immediate actions a governance committee can take to identify quality board directors.

1. Train other committee chairs on the use of leadership assessment tools. You don't want to bury your chairs with unnecessary paperwork, but you do want their input on those committee members who demonstrate leadership qualities.

2. Survey your shareholders (volunteers, staff, vendors, clients of your services) and ask for board director recommendations. Be sure to provide a copy of board director responsibilities. You will receive the right mix of internal and external potential candidates.

3. Invite senior staff members to join a working committee as an ex-officio. This individual can serve two purposes. First, they can provide valuable insight into the leadership qualities of the committee chair. Second, this individual can provide the committee with big picture information about the nonprofits successes and challenges.

4. Charge the Governance Committee to develop a skill matrix identifying specific skills that the board will need in the future (1 -5 years out) to carry out the strategic plan or to provide advice on operational deficiencies.

5. Charge the Governance Committee with the task of carrying out an annual board evaluation. Board evaluations are essential for measuring the current skill levels and identifying missing skills. Getting the right mix of expertise and thinking can make the difference between an capable board and an incompetent one. Just as important as the annual evaluation is a brief assessment at the conclusion of each board meeting. This could be a written statement submitted to the chair within five days of the meeting close or a two-minute briefing per board director. When a written statement is used, the board chair should present a brief summary at the next meeting during the training session. Individual

oral statements should be summarized in the board minutes. The results of self-assessments should identify strategic areas of focus by the board over the next year or two.

In creating a healthy board, it is important to recruit directors who have a variety of experiences and skills in the nonprofit's service area and in the business arena. Diversity is not just about race and gender. The board needs diversity in thinking as well. That means finding your biggest critics and inviting them to join the board. As CEO you might need to convince the chair about the benefits of diversity. Show the chair the board compositions of successful nonprofits. Invite the chair of one of these organizations to have a discussion with your chair. Establishing a diverse board will make your life as CEO much better and productive.

Because the board holds the ultimate fiduciary responsibility of the nonprofit, it is essential that the board composition consists of at least one financial expert (a banker, chief financial officer, an accountant, or another finance manager). It is also advisable to have an attorney on board as well as a marketing/branding expert. Having a diverse board reduces the risk that the board as a whole will make costly legal and business mistakes. If for some reason you are not able to create a diverse board of industry experts, consider creating a small advisory board of business experts. Warning, though. If you do create an advisory board be prepared to share in detail and absolute truth the issues that keep you awake at night. Also be prepared to follow their advice. Remember these folks are busy professionals who are willing to give up their time to help your cause. Treat them with the utmost respect and understand that any advice they offer is in the best interests of the nonprofit.

One topic to remember when developing a healthy board either through recruitment or training is respect. Directors do not have to like each other, but they do need to accept that all directors are on the board for one common goal - to help the nonprofit deliver on its mission. However, there is one exception. It is important to recognize that toxic individuals suck the oxygen out of every room they enter. Regardless of the skills they may possess, avoid nominating venomous individuals to the board. A healthy culture is far more important than talent. Skills can be learned, borrowed or bought. One weed can destroy an entire garden. Be vigilant about protecting board culture. Be sure to have a written board policy on board behavior and the removal of board directors. Many boards fail to create this policy and suffer the consequences.

One of the most frustrating aspects of recruiting quality board directors is all of the hooplas that nonprofits make potential candidates go through. Generally, a candidate must have served the nonprofit as a volunteer leader in some capacity with a variety of committees. Only after many years of involvement is one eligible for board director nomination. There is a major problem with this approach. That being, the reliance on long-standing internally grown candidates who may lack the qualities and skills needed by the board. Newer and younger volunteers, as well as qualified non-volunteers outside of the nonprofit, are dismissed because they haven't put in the right amount of time. The rationale is time served equals qualified board director. This is just wrong-headed thinking. Time is a value of quantity, not quality. Serving many years on volunteer committees may indicate an individual's level of patience and ambition, but gives no indication of the degree of leadership skills. Unfortunately, over the years I have witnessed many board directors who have come through the internal process and were unfit stewards of the organization.

2. Audit Committee

Every nonprofit regardless of its size should have an annual audit conducted by a competent accounting firm. It is important that the nonprofit has adequate internal controls over all financial matters.

The role of the audit committee is to ensure that an independent auditor (no employee or benefit generating relationships with the nonprofit) is qualified and selected to perform the audit. The audit committee meets with the auditor prior to the audit to establish the overall audit plan – what will be and what will not be audited. Once the audit is completed, the audit committee meets again with the auditor to review the results of the audit and overall review of the financial statements. Generally, the auditor will make recommendations on how to improve internal controls, financial reporting, GAPP procedures, or off-balance sheet transactions. The two areas most likely to be mentioned are revenue recognition and expense accounting. The Audit Committee should engage the auditor with any difficulties they may have encountered performing the audit, were any irregularities discovered, and come to a clear understanding of the nonprofits financial status. Once the audit is completed, and all meetings have been held, the Audit Committee will report back to the full board at the next regularly scheduled meeting. Many times, the Audit Committee will recommend to the board a management action plan to be implemented by the CEO. This is a good thing because it allows the board to fulfill its fiduciary duties while providing the CEO with a clear path for managing the organization's finances.

3. Executive Director / CEO Evaluation Committee

Only four out of ten executive directors receive an annual performance evaluation by their boards. And six out of ten nonprofits have no written CEO performance appraisal plan for the CEO. This is not good for the CEO and bad for the nonprofit organization. The CEO evaluation is an important communication tool for the CEO. The evaluation process engages both the board and CEO in active participation and discussion about nonprofit goals and vision. It's an opportunity to set agreed upon goals, to discuss challenges and opportunities. The evaluation is an opportunity for the CEO to shed the isolation of leadership and create a constructive partnership with the board.

Feedback is an essential part of transparent leadership. The CEO needs to keep the board informed of ongoing successes and challenges and vice versa. No one likes bad surprises. With that in mind, there are three functions of the CEO Evaluation Committee. They are: (1) establish priorities on which formal evaluation will be based; (2) meet informally with CEO quarterly and; (3) conduct the formal evaluation.

For the first part, the CEO and CEO Evaluation Committee meet and discuss where they want the nonprofit to be one year from now. From that discussion, priorities are established and written into an action plan. Some of the typical topics include:

- What measurements and key performance indicators (KPI) will be used to evaluate program and service performance?
- What key issues need to be resolved during the next twelve months?
- Any questions either party has about staffing needs.
- Any questions about resource allocation.
- Questions or changes required in the formal evaluation instrument.

Essentially, the CEO evaluation process is about establishing the information sources the committee needs and the resources the CEO requires to move the nonprofit forward in meeting the wishes of its clients.

Developing and maintaining a strong CEO / Board relationship requires continual communication. Quarterly discussions between the CEO and Evaluation Committee about progress, challenges, and trends is a good way to build positive relationships. It's a good way to resolve issues as they arise before tensions (on both sides) fester into something ugly.

The formal evaluation instrument should be a tool agreed to by both the CEO and the Evaluation Committee. Key components of the document should include the topics of, mission, vision, strategy, communication, and board relationship. While some evaluation forms can be exhaustive and complicated, the only purpose of the document is to help the CEO lead the organization in an effective and efficient manner. Don't get too complicated. The evaluation should measure only goals and priorities that are important to the organization.

Many, if not most evaluation forms use a numerical system to evaluate the CEO. If possible, stay away from numbers. Words from the committee will provide more guidance than a subjective and meaningless number. A rating of 4.5 out of 5 may sell books on Amazon, but it has no real meaning to a CEO, other than he/she is not perfect. Words, on the other hand, can be specific and describe accomplishments as well as disappointments while providing concrete actions for the future. And that is what the formal evaluation is all about – the future. The formal evaluation sets the CEO priorities for next twelve months.

4. Budget Committee

The role of the budget committee is to work with the CFO and CEO to develop an action plan for both revenue generation and operational expenses for the next fiscal year. The most important element for the committee to keep in mind is the ability of the nonprofit to deliver on mission and vision as outlined in the strategic plan. Future goals rather than past accomplishments must rule the day. Here are a few tips to keep in mind when developing the budget.

- The CEO should arrange multiple times for the budget committee to meet (phone conference) with program managers and CFO. The committee needs to have a thorough understanding of where revenue comes from, when it comes in, and what expenses are incurred delivering the mission.
- Create an annual schedule, or timeline, for when documents need to be completed and by who.
- Using the strategic plan as a guide, establish (in priority order) mission goals.
- Require program managers to estimate all resources (human and capital) needed to fulfill each identified mission goal. Estimates should also include all projected revenue associated with each mission goal.
- The Budget Committee, in concert with the CEO, will then need to make decisions as to what will be funded and what will be discontinued. When decisions are made, a preliminary budget can be constructed for full board review and approval.
- When presenting the initial budget to the full board, it is best done by the Budget Committee. These are the colleagues of the board, the group the board entrusted the responsibility for budget oversight. If the right directors are on the committee and the CEO has done

his/her job correctly with providing the committee accurate operational details the message should be well-received.

5. Investment Committee

The role of the Investment Committee is similar to that of the Budget Committee except that they will work with the nonprofit's outside investment manager. The most important duty of the Investment Committee is to develop an investment policy statement. The statement should be a set of guidelines rather than a strict set of rules. The investment manager can help the committee with this as he/she will have a full understanding of market conditions and trends. The committee should meet with the advisor quarterly.

If the nonprofit does not have an investment portfolio, find a way to create one. Just as one puts a little money aside each month for retirement, the nonprofit must put aside something for future growth and survival.

Leadership Succession Plan

The nonprofit executive director is the organization's chief executive officer. As such, the executive director is the paid staff member who is responsible for all operational decisions. The executive director develops and manages the budget, hires and fires all staff, develops and evaluates programs, implements board decisions, must have strong business savvy, understand basic marketing, and have good public relations skills to name a few. The point is, the executive director oversees every aspect of the nonprofit and reports only to the board of directors.

The executive director is the most important person in the organization, and as such, must possess the skill set needed to move the organization forward as dictated by the strategic plan and vision. Yet, as many as 75 percent of all nonprofits have no written succession plan or a leadership development plan. This is problematic as more and more executive directors leave their positions suddenly. Some studies have reported that fewer than half of all nonprofit directors were satisfied with their current position. Other surveys reported that nearly one-third of all newly appointed nonprofit executive directors plan on staying on the job for less than two years because of lack of support from the board that hired them. That leaves many insecure executives leading nonprofits. It also leads to executive director decisions made for self-preservation reasons rather than what might be in the best interest of the organization. None of this is good for the executive director or the nonprofit.

Every board should have a leadership sustainability plan, designed with input from the CEO, in place to handle planned and unplanned vacancies in leadership. In the case of the CEO's sudden departure from the organization, the board will want to hire an interim executive director. While a board may be tempted to promote another executive from the ranks of the current nonprofit, they should resist this impulse. The board will need time to evaluate future goals against future skills of an executive director. Putting the right person in place will take time. Employing an independent, third-party interim for a period of 9 to 15 months allows the nonprofit to continue to deliver on its mission while giving the board the opportunity to conduct a proper and thorough executive search. Promoting an existing employee to the executive's office can cause many other unintended and unwelcomed consequences. Even if the board announces the promotion as a temporary move, many in and around the organization may view the move as a precursor to a permanent appointment. When a final decision is made, and the interim is not selected it may be difficult for the interim to return to his former position as not every decision made during the interim period may be popular with staff, especially if significant changes were necessary to keep the organization afloat. The interim may also feel embarrassed and hurt when not appointed as the permanent executive director and decide to leave the organization. Any employee worthy of being selected as an interim executive director is an employee the organization wants and needs to keep.

As in the case of the board chair leaving unexpectedly, the board should have a well-developed policy detailing how the board will select an interim executive director along with term limits. It would be a good idea to cite a few management companies that provide interim executives in the policy. The policy should also prohibit current board members from filling the role of interim as that may be a violation of the Intermediate Sanctions Excess Benefit Section of the IRS – a fineable offense to both the board and the director who would serve as the interim.

CHAPTER TWO

The CEO

Becoming a CEO of a nonprofit is a life-changing event. In addition to managing your relationship with the board, success as CEO will greatly depend on the relationships you build with staff. It is important that you develop and empower employees to act independently to deliver mission goals. Hold them accountable but give them the tools and resources they do to perform their job. Active employee participation at all levels is essential to continuous improvement and quality execution of products and services offered by the nonprofit. Empowered employees are how a CEO translates strategy into organizational capabilities.

One, if not the most important things a CEO should do is build an open and trusting culture. The CEO needs to create an emotionally safe climate in which staff feels comfortable taking risks acquired from experiences and knowledge of the organization. To do this, the CEO must be open to:

- asking and receiving questions
- openly exchange ideas and challenges with staff
- giving and receiving candid feedback
- communicating ideas in a clear and transparent manner about goals and vision

- maintaining a strategic focus on the client and ways to improve services and products

A positive culture drives everything; it drives success. The organization needs to be a place where people want to come to work and solve problems. It is the CEO's responsibility to create the conditions that enable staff and the board to create value for the clients. That means allowing the staff closest to a problem to make decisions to resolve the conflict. It involves teamwork, collaboration, and the sharing of data and accountability. The CEO needs to train staff to ask questions that challenge ideas and facts to improve products or services. (Criticizing and blaming are harmful and should be avoided at all levels of management.) This is hard work, but leadership is all about making good workers better. Leadership is about building learning into every part of the organization.

As CEO you must also understand that the nonprofit must continually adapt to new situations, therefore learning new practices must coexist with executing current procedures. Teamwork is a valuable tool for assisting organizational growth. It is not necessary to form actual teams for every task. Rather, encourage staff to share their knowledge and challenges, with other employees. Just the act of communicating and collaborating informally with colleagues across departments and divisions is an effective way for staff to develop new expertise and skills. The more capabilities your staff has, the more impactful your services and products will become.

The CEO will be expected to demonstrate strong operational discipline. There are many good books on quality management techniques. Be sure to find time to read books and professional journals on leadership and management. You can't do this job alone. Lean on others and their experiences so that you may continue to grow as a CEO. But understand you are the steward of organizational value. Preserving and creating new value means getting you people ready for future challenges. That starts with the CEO being ready.

Managing Board Meetings

The board meeting is the number one source of interaction between the CEO and Board Directors. It is the place where Board Directors will judge and evaluate the CEO's skills, behavior, and capabilities as a leader. Regardless of who runs the meeting, the CEO should ensure it is structured in an efficient and effective manner. This includes the availability of all meeting materials. When the meeting is over the CEO wants the Board to feel good about how their time was spent.

In preparing for a board meeting, the CEO should:

- Ten days prior to the meeting schedule calls with the board chair and officers to discuss key issues that will be reported on in CEO report. This can eliminate surprises during the meeting – surprises that can derail both the tone and context of the meeting.
- Send out the board agenda with all key information updates after board officer calls have been completed, but no later than five days prior to the meeting. This gives directors enough time to prepare for strategic discussions.
- Develop a PowerPoint deck of graphs forecasts, or other items related to the agenda – send the deck to the board with the agenda.
- Board Agenda Structure
  - Two strategic topics for discussion and debate – 80% of the meeting (maximize time to discuss the issues that are most vital).
  - Information needed to make good decisions – up to 10% of the meeting. (If necessary)

- o Voting on the main issues and other administrative items – up to 10% of the meeting. (If necessary)

- Remember, the purpose of the meeting is about setting the course for future direction and not about reading information reports that directors can read on their own time (prior to the meeting).

The Meeting

- All board directors should show up at the meeting prepared to participate (meaning they have read all board materials prior to the meeting).
- A good board will also want to establish a framework for board discussions. This is necessary because it is easy to talk forever on a topic without ever actually coming to a conclusion. This is commonly known as paralysis by analysis. Appointing different board directors (prior to meeting agenda distribution to directors) to lead each topic would help keep discussions on target.
- Keep meeting focused on top strategic topics.
- Questions unrelated to the strategic issues should be delayed to the end of the meeting, providing time permits.
- After the meeting, the CEO should write up a set of unofficial notes from his/her perception of the meeting and send to the board as soon as possible for verification of main discussion points and decisions. These notes are not part of the official board minutes, but rather a personal communication from CEO to board to ensure everyone is on the same page.

Between Board Meetings

- CEO should send update notes to board on an agreed upon schedule – every two weeks, three weeks max.

- The board should use committees of the board to do the work of the board. The CEO should work with committee chairs to establish a schedule of planned conference calls and agendas to do the work. Try to limit calls to 45 minutes or less every two to three weeks – if needed. The CEO should provide each committee member with a brief summary prior to the next scheduled phone meeting. For documents, use Dropbox or some other storage sharing software.

A Word about Hiring a CEO

When searching for a new CEO, board directors have a tendency to look for someone just like the current or former CEO. This is a mistake. The current CEO may have been the right choice at the time of their hiring, but chances are the nonprofit now needs a different set of skills. Hire for future growth rather than for past accomplishments that do not connect with future needs. If you are a current CEO and retirement is nearing, take time to discuss this with the board. If you are ready to search for CEO position use this knowledge to convince a hiring board to want the skills that you possess.

Professional membership nonprofits – especially education and health related – have a tendency to look for the next CEO from that profession. There are quite a number of nonprofits that require the CEO to hold a Ph.D. in the profession. This is short-sighted thinking as it dramatically reduces the pool of potential candidates. Consider the number of Ph.D.'s in a particular field who want to be CEO of a nonprofit. The number will be small. Then consider the number of Ph.D.'s who possess the executive level knowledge, training, and experiences. The number will be insignificant. Just remember, the CEO will perform executive duties. They will not perform surgery, take your blood pressure (although their job performance may cause it to spike), conduct a research project, or do your tax return.

Hire for the executive skills needed and not for expertise in a specific and narrow field.

If you use the title of Executive Director, I recommend you change it to Chief Executive Officer (CEO) to reflect the reality and importance of the job. There is another reason to change the name. Many for-profit companies now use the title of Executive Director in their management hierarchy. In the corporate environment, the executive director is a position that falls underneath the level of vice-president and is similar to the position of project manager. In order to help the nonprofit CEO negotiate the best possible agreements and contracts, it would be wise to award the title (CEO) to communicate to all that this executive is the top dog.

Survival Tips for a New or Seasoned CEO

1. Surprise! This job is not like your previous job. There is no safety net, no supervisor above you to bail you out of a wrong decision. Use multiple sources of data to make informed decisions. Own your decisions even if they go south.
2. You own every decision made throughout the organization. Train all employees in effective decision-making strategies.
3. The CEO is a very public job. You are under intense scrutiny from everyone, both in and out of the organization. Everything you do, say, or wear will be talked about. Speak well, behave as if you were in church, and dress consistently. Exude a calm demeanor, and people will soon have confidence in you.
4. Don't criticize or speak ill of the former leadership. You want to win over followers, not alienate those who believed in the former leader.
5. Get out of your office every day. Walk the floor and talk to staff – all staff. Ask about their challenges and what

you can do to help them. Make yourself known to the clients you serve, talk to them. Don't forget to reach out to all board members. Regular contact with them is key to CEO success.

6. Leading is hard – you carry responsibility for the entire organization on your back. You can't do it alone. Develop a cadre of capable insiders and outsiders who can help you accomplish organizational goals.

7. If possible, find a mentor. Someone who has been a successful CEO who understands what leadership means, someone who is willing to advise you when needed.

8. Communicate clearly and often with the people who report directly to you. Listen to them. Help them find solutions to their most pressing problems. Share your ideas and management traits with them. Most importantly, help them to feel like a valuable member of the team (which they are).

9. Remember to thank people.

10. Manage your time, or it will manage you. Schedule a set daily time for responding to emails, for phone calls, for walking the floor. Time is the only resource you can't add to or subtract from.

11. Start and end meetings on time. This shows respect for attendees' time. Prepare and circulate an agenda well before a meeting enabling staff to come prepared.

12. Build and maintain strong business partnerships with other nonprofits, government agencies, and corporations.

CHAPTER THREE

Developing Employees as Leaders

The goal of this chapter of the book is to help the CEO turn every employee into a leader, someone who:

(a) Has the ability to collect multiple sources of organizational data and client community information
(b) Can extract insights from that information and work experience to make sound decisions about his/her work
(c) Can effectively communicate those decisions to co-workers and supervisors, and
(d) Can contribute to a culture where everyone creates client community value –horizontal and vertically

The benefits of leadership development are:

a) Staff becomes the center of organizational problem solving
b) Everyone working on the same organizational page – employees, actions, organizational goals, and results are connected
c) Strategic thinking becomes part of everyone, everyday thinking and doing
d) Healthy culture of accountability and transparency

e) Happy, engaged, and productive employees who learn from each other

Chances are, many of your employees may not know if or how their work contributes to or hinders the organization's mission. If that is the case, how effective can your organization be in delivering its services? If your staff routinely does what they have always done and don't know why it's always been done this way; they are not thinking about, or doing, the right things to help your organization. According to the Harvard Business Review,[2] 85% of executives spend less than one hour per month discussing strategy; 50% spend no time. If management is not talking about strategy, chances are the rank and file employee; those who put the strategy into action do not know the organization's strategy. If the staff doesn't know the big picture strategy, how effective can they be in implementing the strategy? Not very.

Should your employees spend most of their time recreating past actions, essentially working on autopilot? Putting out today's brush fires? Of course, we know the answer to these questions are no. We do not want our employees following Einstein's Theory of Insanity. We need employees – from top to bottom – who can innovate; who can solve tomorrow's problems today; who can drive your organization forward effortlessly, efficiently, and effectively.

Working as one organization means all employees. must know why the organization exists; what it stands for; how it conducts business; who are its clients, and how each employee contributes to organizational success. Each employee should by using their expertise to make the thoughtful decisions of today that will shape tomorrow's organization. When all employees

---

[2] "The office of Strategic Management." Kaplan & Norton. *Harvard Business Review*. October 2005

understand the organization, its clients, and how their job impacts the future of that organization, the organization is working in synch and improves its chances of making sustained and impactful contributions to the mission and people it serves. So how do you transform, or institutionalize, strategic leadership into everyday practice?

Let's start by thinking about why the organization exists. Why is this important? If you want your team to operate at full potential, to reach new heights continuously, and to enjoy a sustainable future, all of your employees need to understand why the organization exists fully. Each employee must fully understand the organization's mission and vision for the future in order to be fully engaged in shaping that future. If mission and vision are cloudy, organizational confusion and resistance will be present. Once employees understand completely why the organization exists, they can align their resources and work decisions to match the mission and vision.

What Each Employee Must Know About Mission

- What does the organization do? And for who? (the clients of your services)
- How does this work benefit society?
- How does the organization make the world better?
- How does each program contribute to making the world better?
- How does each department contribute to making the world better?
- How do individual employees contribute to departmental and organizational program success that make the world a better place?

To address these questions, the CEO should insist that every employee has a copy of the organization's mission statement visible at their workstation. This serves as a daily reminder of why the organization exists and has staff. It also reminds employees of what will be measured to determine organizational impact.

Review your mission statement annually. It should be short, plainspoken, and clearly state what (not how) the organization has set out to accomplish. Shorter is better – think slogan. Your mission statement should focus only on what impact that can be measured.

Well-Written Mission Statement	*Rehabilitate houses in South Central Chicago for low-income tenants.*
Poorly Written Mission Statement	*At XYZ, we wish to make the world a better place by nurturing each human beings' capacity to build happy, meaningful, and productive lives*

Notice the difference between the two examples. The poorly written statement is not measurable while the well-written statement can be measured. You cannot fix what you cannot measure.

Organizational Exercise 1	CHALLENGE: Can your organization create a mission statement in 10 words or less? Give it a try; you won't regret it.

Vision Statement

In addition to the mission statement, every employee should be familiar with the vision statement. Questions employees should be able to answer:

- What is the preferred future of the organization?
- Do our current programs take us to the future?

- How does each department take us to the preferred future?
- How does the individual employee make a difference?

Just like the mission statement, every employee should have a copy of the organization's vision statement visible at their workstation.   Developing a meaningful vision (& vision statement) is one of the most difficult, but important, tasks for any organization. When it comes to planning, human beings tend to be more comfortable looking in the rear view mirror for ideas rather than imagining what lies over the horizon. Be careful that your vision is not simply an extension of past activities. Your vision statement needs to be forward looking, imagining what the perfect scenario might look like.

The vision statement must focus on the organization's core competencies; what it does best now and will continue to excel at in the future. How will the organization use its core competencies to deliver its mission three, five, or seven years from now? Think JFK and putting a man on the moon as a guide.

Well-Written Vision Statement	*A hunger-free Chicago*
Poorly Written Vision Statement	*Develop, deploy, and manage a diverse set of scalable and strategic knowledge management tools to serve our clients, improving the possibility of overall life satisfaction.*

Notice the difference between the two examples. ..The poorly written statement is too complex and fails to deliver on specific ideas. The well-written statement tells the world exactly what the nonprofit wants to do.

Organizational Exercise 2	CHALLENGE: Can your organization create an impact-driven vision statement that excites your stakeholders about the future? Give it a try.

Describe organization's updated vision:

- How will this change or improve mission delivery?
- How will this change benefit the client community & staff?

Organizational Exercise 3	CHALLENGE: Test your vision statement. Answer the following five questions with a yes, no, or maybe. Yes is good. No, and maybe indicate you have some work to do in defining a workable vision statement. 1. Is your vision compelling? 2. Is your vision realistic? 3. Is your vision manageable? 4. Is your vision easy to communicate? 5. Is your vision future focused?

What Every Employee Must Know What About Values

All organizations have principles, or values, that guide decision making. Guiding principles are passed along by word of mouth, leadership actions, or are present in a written document. Implicit or explicit, these principles impact organizational outcomes. How the organization interacts with itself and with the outside world will determine how successful the organization is in fulfilling its mission. If the staff doesn't know what the organization values, how effective can they be in implementing the strategy? Questions the CEO should focus on:

- What does the organization value?
- How do organizational principles transform day-to-day activities into success or failure?
- How are employees responsible for adhering to organizational values with decisions they make?

The CEO should require each employee to receive a copy of the Statement of Core Values, sometimes referred to as Guiding Principles, once a year. They should be asked to sign a receipt acknowledging a willingness to adhere to values. The nonprofit's clients should have access to your Statement of Core Values published on your web and newsletters.

Reviewing Current Statement of Core Values

1. Survey your employees to determine their understanding of the organization's values – do they know them? Incorporate them in decision making?
2. If you have a written Statement of Core Values revisit, revise against following criteria:
   a. Focus on behavior – how we interact with other employees, client community, vendors, and outside partners
   b. Focus on core values that already exist within the organization
   c. Govern how employees. act – with others and in daily decision making
   d. Two to three core values and no more. The more core values you have, the more difficult it is for employees to (1) live up to those values and (2) make good decisions based on the core values
3. Review all operational policies, including HR, IT, budgeting, marketing, and client community policies against values

Developing a Statement of Core Values

1. Convene a small senior management working group (five to seven) representing respected managers from different functions across the organization – include the CEO.

2. Challenge the group to identify and define a set of core values that the organization must adhere to at all times.

3. Core values must focus on behavior –how we interact with other employees, client community, vendors, and outside partners.

4. Focus on core values that already exist within the organization rather than something you have to create - what current values does the organization reward?

5. Core values govern how employees act – with others and in daily decision making.

6. You should end up with two to three core values and no more. The more core values you have, the more difficult, it is for employees to:
   a. Live up to those values and
   b. Make sound decisions based on the core values

7. After identifying the core values, create a chart, or narrative, that show examples of core values in use.

8. When a set of core values has been identified and defined, send the list out, with a chart of examples, to all employees and board members. Ask all to think about the ways they demonstrate the use of core values on a daily basis, or how they can use the core values to improve their work practice. This exercise gives all employees an opportunity to connect with the core values and discussion around core values should be part of regularly scheduled staff meetings.

9. Request board approval core values at the next board meeting

10. When approved, distribute the final version to all employees and board members. Ask for a signature of acceptance of Statement of Core Values.

11. Distribute Statement of Core Values to the client community via the web, newsletters, emails, social media, etc. Attach a copy of Statement of Core Values to all vendor agreements and contracts.

Transform Day-To-Day Activities Using Values

1. Embed value statements into work processes, procedures, planning

2. Build value statements discussions into departmental meetings

3. Review projects against both strategy and core values

4. Incorporate value statements into organizational, departmental, and employee evaluations

5. Align policies, vendor agreements, etc. with statement of values

6. Require each department to share projects with each other so all can see what and how work is being performed

7. Charge your supervisors and managers to keep core values as part of the day-to-day dialogue with employees.

Having a written Statement of Core Values does not guarantee organizational commitment to values. All employees must live the values as easily as they breathe in air. The CEO must help employees embrace the core values: all employees must understand they will be held accountable for:

- Both **what** and **how** they **perform**
- Caring about people as much as the mission

Exhibit 1 Signs of a Positive Work Culture

1. People smile often – high morale
2. Communications at all levels and between all levels are frequent and presented in a constructive and cordial manner – there is minimal organizational confusion
3. Change is not feared
4. Minimal organizational (at all levels) politics interfering with work
5. Managers welcome and encourage challenges to ideas
6. Managers redirect when mistakes are made rather than admonish
7. Successes are celebrated
8. Everyone knows each other's name
9. Gossip is the water cooler is about last night's reality show rather than about other employees.'
10. Employees seem to like their jobs, their colleagues, and the client community who they serve
11. When issues or conflicts arise, they are handled quickly and openly rather than swept under the carpet.
12. High productivity is evident at all levels

Exhibit 2 Sample of Core Values Statement

INTEGRITY

Examples of integrity:

- Transparency – no organizational secrets
- Hold ourselves and others accountable
- Honest dealings with co-workers, vendors, members
- Humble
- Do you best work even when no one is looking

Examples NOT showing integrity

- Public embarrass co-worker, vendor, member
- Tell people what you think they want to hear
- Do just enough to get by

COMPASSION

Examples of Compassion

- Treat co-workers, client community, vendors with respect
- Respond in a timely manner to requests from all
- Looks others in the eyes when listening
- Smile and say "Hi" to others

Examples NOT showing compassion

- Use pejorative language when speaking with others
- Always complete tasks and requests later rather than sooner
- Read text messages on your smart phone when someone is addressing you
- Answer your cell phone when in the middle of a conversation with someone

Employees Must Know the Business Model

During the course of a football game, the offense will huddle, and the quarterback will call a play. Each play is designed to achieve positive yards, and each player has an assigned role. In order to score points, each player must understand how the offense scores points. They must understand why players need to be in certain positions, what they will do once the ball is in play, and trust that everyone will be where they are required to be. This is particularly the case during a down-field passing play where the receiver must run to where the ball will be. It is the job of the entire offense to ensure players get to where the ball will be. The same is true for the nonprofit. Each employee must understand how the organization scores points.

What Employee Must Know about Business Model

Your organization's business model is different from the organization's strategy. The business model is about the processes, procedures, and activities used to produce client value and revenue for the organization. Questions to answer.

- How does the organization deliver services and products to clients?
- How does the organization create value for the client? This includes pricing, marketing, HR, IT, administration, and customer service.
- Does the current infrastructure support your business model in the most efficient way possible?
- Do employees understand resource limitations?
- Do employees understand that the organization cannot be all things to all clients?
- What is the organization's capacity to deliver services/programs now and in the future?

The questions sound simple, but chances are your staff does not understand your business model – how you create value for the client and revenue for the organization.

What every employee needs to know about your organization's business model:

- Client value - what services and products do the organization produce to solve society or client problems?
- Expenses – to understand organizational costs you must understand both direct costs and indirect costs across all program and service areas and across geographic sites if your organization has more than one physical location. Traditional nonprofit and small business accounting breaks down indirect costs by functions (administration, marketing, accounting, public relations, etc.) rather than by programs failing to capture the relationship between costs and organizational activities. Indirect costs associated with programs must be known.
- Revenue – where does the money come from? It is important to know how much revenue is produced by each program, product, service, and funding source.

Revenue & Financial Statements

A big part of understanding the business model includes a basic understanding of where all revenue comes from, seasonal changes in cash flow, and how expenses are incurred. Your CFO will want to give some basic training to staff on the reading of financial statements. Managers and supervisors should include a review of financial statements during regularly scheduled departmental meetings. Of particular importance will be discussions of direct costs vs. indirect costs, revenue vs. net revenue, accrual vs. cash accounting, and how the accounting department allocates 100 percent of time & money.

Helping Employee Understand Where Money Comes From and Where It Goes

The CEO should ensure that every employee has a copy and understands the basics of the following:

Statement of Financial Position – snapshot of organizational financial health (assets & liabilities) at a fixed point in time

- Shows all current organizational assets, might include: accounts receivable, land & buildings, equipment, long-term investments, work in progress
- Shows all current organizational liabilities, might include: accounts payable, payroll, lease contracts, taxes
- Shows where organization is financially strong/weak

Statement of Financial Activities – compares program revenue against expenses for a particular point in time –month, quarter, etc.

- Shows month by month financial successes and weaknesses
- Shows revenue and expenses on a monthly basis
- A good tool for comparing previous year's results to this year's results month by month –identify revenue and expense trends

Statement of Cash Flow – will show the cash flow cycle

- When cash comes in & when cash goes out of the organization
- Use the indirect method of showing cash flow to get a full understanding of the effect of net income on cash balance
- Will show net cash from operating and investment activities

Organizational Exercise 4

CHALLENGE: Can your organization use its financial statements to forecast future program revenues and expenses?
CHALLENGE: Can your senior team quickly identify your organization's primary inputs, activities, outputs, and outcomes?
CHALLENGE: Can all of your employees articulate how all organizational work fits together to create client value?

Although not a financial barometer of overall organizational performance, you might find it very useful to create a Statement of Departmental Expenses comparing previous year expenses/revenues to current year for each program. This statement should be very detailed and include all expenses and revenues with a year-to-year variance. This tool allows program managers and staff to carefully monitor and question performance with the option for in-year corrections to the program. There is nothing worse than waiting until the end of the budget year only to find particular aspects of the program went awry. Things that could of and should have been fixed at the point of discovery. A Modified Statement of Functional Expenses may also be helpful.

Direct vs. Indirect Expense

Direct costs are connected to one program or service offered by the organization.

Examples of direct costs include:

- Salaries and benefits for staff members working exclusively on the program
- Travel expenses and equipment costs attributable to only the staff members who work on the program

- Supplies and materials for the program
- Vendor or contractor fees for the program

Indirect costs are costs shared across more than one program and are often referred to as overhead.

Examples of indirect costs include:

- Any expenses that are not directly connected to a particular program and have not been identified as a direct cost
- General administration and management expenses (salaries and benefits)
- Infrastructure costs (rent, utilities, equipment depreciation, software licenses)
- Any costs that are incurred for the benefit of all the programs within the organization such as marketing costs, advocacy expenses, public relations, the board of directors meetings.

A word about Indirect Costs (Overhead) Allocation Methods. There are four basic methods to allocate expenses. Most common include:

1. Square footage
2. Time
3. Actual usage
4. Percentage of direct costs

How to Use Square Footage Allocation Method

- Calculate the percentage of total square footage each program uses against total organizational square footage
- Use square foot percentage to divide the overhead
- Each program will have different indirect costs dependent of square footage used by program

How to Use Time Allocation Method
- Total hours each employee puts into a program
- Determine percentage of total man-hours the program demands
- Ex. If program A uses 25% of your staff's time, it gets 25% of the overhead budget
- If you use this method, 100% employee time must be accounted for through time sheets

How to Use Actual Usage Allocation Method
- Relies on actual rate of direct cost usage by each program to determine indirect cost
- If program incurs 25% of all direct costs, it is assigned 25% of all indirect costs

How to Use Percentage of Direct Costs Allocation Method
- A percentage determined by dividing the amount of the direct expenses of each program by the total expenses of the organization
- Ex. A fixed percentage, say 22%, is added to all program direct costs to determine total program expense

Knowing the Client
Every employee should be aware who your client community is – your market. Whether you call them customers, clients, or members – why do these individuals spend time and money with your organization? Finding ways to engage employees. with the client community is essential for understanding why they chose your organization. Questions to be answered.

- What are the external factors pressing against your client community?
- What trends might have positive or negative consequences on your client community?

- What is the big problem your client community is trying to solve? Is that problem shrinking, growing, staying the same?
- How big is your client community? Is it stable, growing, shrinking?
- What keeps your clients engaged with your organization?

Organizational Exercise 5	CHALLENGE: If you had 60 minutes to pick the brains of your client avatar, what are some key questions you would want to ask him/her that would help the nonprofit become more relevant, impactful, or meaningful? Discuss staff rationale for question-making.

Create a Client Avatar to Help Staff to Know Client

What is a client avatar? A client avatar is a composite of individuals who use your services. You may have more than one product or service and will want to develop an avatar for each unique service or product you provide. Give each avatar a name and a picture that represents the characteristics of the avatar. Create a shortly written fact sheet of your ideal client, be as specific as you can be. Answering as many of the following questions should help:

- What does your avatar do for a living and what is his income?
- Where does your avatar live? What sort of house and area does he live in?
- What does your avatar spend her money on?
- How old is your avatar?
- What kind of education does your avatar have?
- What is your avatar's marital status?

- Does your avatar have children? How many?
- What does your avatar enjoy doing in her spare time?
- What does your avatar like and dislike?
- What is your avatar's top fear or frustration?
- What keeps your avatar awake at night?
- What does your avatar want from your organization?
- What questions does your avatar ask most often?

After you have developed avatar of your client community, you will want to review how your organization's fit with the avatar's most pressing needs. Answer the following questions:

1. What are some of the signs that the avatar is loyal to our organization?
2. What steps are we currently taking to foster avatar loyalty?
3. What additional steps could we be taking?
4. What steps could we take to attract more avatar? Think of what you might do in the following areas:
   a. Marketing
   b. Product development
   c. Accounting & finance
   d. Membership
5. What additional resources, training or other support would help you meet or exceed your avatar's expectations?

Engaging Employees with Client Community

- Conduct a client community benefit audit to see which services/products are really delivering value in the minds of the client. Survey Monkey is a cheap and effective way to conduct the audit. You don't need to ask many questions, just relevant ones that tell how the community feel about your services and products

- Create continuous feedback loop with clients and employees.
- Ask clients how they want to be communicated with by the organization
- Continually monitor services/products from a client viewpoint. What are they experiencing when they come to you?
- Tune into your client community professional resources – journals, meetings, newspaper articles -to stay current with their thinking and insights
- If you have a call center, place non-call center supervisors at a call station one day per month to talk with clients
- Share customer survey summary results with all staff – include good with bad
- Establish an internal system whereby each employee calls one client community member per week only to ask if the client is satisfied with the organization's services & programs
- Encourage employees to join client community committee groups
- Encourage all employees to take ten minutes per week to review comments on organizational social media outlets such as Facebook & Twitter. Reading firsthand accounts of client interests and concerns will increase employees awareness of customer profile
- Conduct focus groups to engage client community in conversations about client needs

Management Communication and Employee Impact

A survey by Booz & Company of 2,800 hundred executives found: "Executives report that their biggest challenges are[3]

a) Ensuring that day-to-day decisions are in line with the strategy (56%) and

b) Allocating resources in a way that really supports the strategy (56%)"

To be effective, every employee must know how their day-to-day work contributes to organizational strategy and mission delivery.

Management, at all levels – especially at the top, cannot repeat organizational vision and strategy enough.

- Consistent and constant management talk of vision and strategy promotes employee interactivity and encourages strategic discussions while keeping employees focused on organizational priorities

- Employees need to know the organization's vision and strategy remain in the forefront of management priorities. Management will need to continue to stress that the vision of the organization is the same vision for every department and employee and that all employees, together, are responsible for organizational success or failure.

- A plan that is clear one day can become cloudy the next. Continuous talk and alignment are necessary to keep organizational priorities in focus.

- In order to make strategic decisions align at all levels of the organization, senior management must be able to tell

---

[3] "Executives Say They're Pulled in Too Many Directions and That Their Company's Capabilities Don't Support Their Strategy." *Booz & Co.* January 18, 2011

the strategy story in a way all staff can connect to their work.

Exhibit 3 Tips for Employee Communication

Over the past decade or two, research has taught us that successful organizations engage all employees in the management of the enterprise. Top down decisions seldom bring positive returns. Rather, it is the routine and continuous contributions of the non-executive employee that brings organizational success.

Tip 1. Managers should make it a regular practice to talk about why the organization exists, what it stands for, how it conducts business, and who it serves. The more employees understand the organization's unique situation, the better they will be able to help the organization prosper and grow.

Tip 2. Train all employees in the fundamentals of organizational finance. Nonexecutive employees make decisions every day – decisions that impact organizational finances. Employees who understand how the organization designates direct vs. indirect costs will be better able to manage both types of costs in their department. Employees who can read and understand the organization's Statements of Financial Position, Financial Activities and Cash Flow will make better decisions now as well as be better prepared to make forecast models of future organizational spending and revenue.

Tip 3. Managers should make it a routine practice to talk about the challenges and trends confronting the organization's client community. What is the big problem facing the client community? What keeps them awake at night? What is the organization doing to help the client community solve the big problem?

Tip 4. Connect all employee work with the mission. Seems like an obvious observation but you might be surprised to learn just how disconnected many employees are to the mission. A 2013 by Gallop found that: only 29% of American workers are actively engaged in their work; 54% are not engaged (lack motivation, not invested in organizational outcomes); and 18% are actively not engaged (unproductive, spread negativity). While we would like to believe that this is not the case in the nonprofit world, we cannot assume the statistics are any different for this class of worker and must address employee connectivity head-on.

Tip 5. Expect every employee to be a leader. Build a culture where information is shared throughout the organization. Hoarding information leads to silo's and can prevent employees. in other departments from making the right decisions for the organizational. Include non-executive employees from all levels in management, communication, and strategy meetings. Encourage employees to communicate with each other, especially those in other departments, and to share insights they have gained from experience and training.

Section I Summary

1. Incompetent board directors reduce the nonprofits value to the community. Competent board directors raise the value. To ensure that the nonprofit has a qualified board engage your current board in governance and finance training often. Remember, they have other full-time jobs and families that require their attention. Training is a way to keep the board informed and to help them understand their obligations to the nonprofit.

2. Manage the board through committees.

3. Structure board meetings with an emphasis on strategic discussions about the future of the organization. Keep the board looking forward rather than in the rear-view mirror. Yesterday is gone and out of reach. The future has yet to be determined.

4. Create an organizational dashboard (web based) to keep the board informed between meetings.

5. Make sure the nonprofit has a CEO succession plan.

6. The Board and CEO must have an active process to address all governance matters.

7. Every nonprofit must have a written policy covering board director nominations, board director term limits, board director ethics and code of conduct, board director conflict of interests, a process for removing negligent board directors, financial transparency, and board director travel and representation of nonprofit.

Four Questions a Board Should Ask the CEO

1. What measures is our organization making to improve its capabilities to deliver on enhance mission?

2. Are our organization's strategy, mission, and vision still in alignment?

3. What are management's assumptions about our organization's future? Looking back over the past three to five years, how well have management's assumptions matched what actually occurred?
4. How effective is our board? Are we recruiting directors with the experience and expertise needed for the board to address the key issues facing our organization?

Five Questions a Nonprofit CEO Should Ask of Self

1. What analytical tools are used to inform the board and are they kept up to date?
2. How do we define program & services success in our organization? Are we sure that definition is aligned with mission and vision?
3. Are we curious enough about our user community? Do we collect enough data often enough from our user community? Do we use it to make decisions?
4. What measures is our organization taking to improve its capabilities to enhance mission delivery?
5. Does the organization have strategic initiatives in place that create opportunities for future strategic choices?

Every employee must have a copy of:

*   Mission Statement
*   Vision Statement
*   Statement of Core Values
*   Financial Statements
    ✓ Statement of Financial Position, Statement of Financial Activities and Statement of Cash Flow

Every employee should have a copy of:

*   Other Financial Documents
    ✓ Statement of Departmental Expenses.
    ✓ Modified Statement of Functional Expenses.

Business Model. - What Employee Must Know

- The problem your organization is trying to solve
- Your unique value – something clients, cannot easily get someplace else
- Your solution - services & products
- How & where do you deliver goods
- Revenue streams
- Cost structure
- Key organizational performance metrics

Every Employee Must Know

- Who is the client community?
- What do they want?
- What do they need?
- Client avatar
- How can we do a better job of meeting client community expectations?
- How does the organization deliver services/products to the client community?
- Are departments aligned with each other?
- Are departments aligned with the organization's strategy?
- Is day-to-day employee work aligned to departmental and organizational goals?

Finance - What Every Employee Must Know

Revenue

- Where does the money come from?
- Does the organization rely on restricted income from investments to support annual operational budget?

Expenses

- Direct vs. indirect costs

- Which programs generate revenue?
- Which programs do not produce revenue?

Departmental Processes, Strategies, and Resources Used

- Do processes and strategies match organizational goals?
- Do resources used match organizational priorities?

Resources Allocation across the Nonprofit

- Are sufficient resources allocated to organizational priorities?
- What are the external factors pressing against your client community?
- What technologies, regulations and training needs are required to impact your clients?

Trends That Might Have Positive or Negative Consequences on the Nonprofit

- Are you aware of current trends in the client community field?
- Strategic thinking is about sharing organizational information, using knowledge & experience to generate insights that lead to good strategic decisions.
- Strategic thinking is about creating an innovative, forward-thinking, collaborative culture where co-workers respect each other, the client community, and a sustainable organization.

Sample Financial Charts

Free Bonus pages can be downloaded at:

https://www.markmullen.org/bonus-pages/

Exhibit 4 Sample Avatar

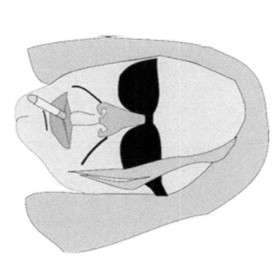

Joe Cool
Age 25

Avatar Profile

~Seasonal construction worker ~ Earns $23,500 per year ~ Lives in suburban trailer park with three roommates; ~Spends $10,500 per year on illegal drugs ~ Dropped out of high school in 11th grade ~In-and-out of romantic relationships, never married ~ Has two children who live with their mothers ~ Plays guitar for fun ~Likes listening to live bands at local bars ~ Dislikes politics and authority ~ Is frustrated by frequent police visits to home responding to noise complaints ~ Biggest fear is he will die young and alone ~Wants you

Figure 1.Sample Statement of Financial Position

STATEMENT OF FINANCIAL POSITION	2014	2013
ASSETS		
Current Assets: Liquidity		
Cash and Equivalents (bank accounts, money-market)		
Accounts Receivable (amounts due from sale of products)		
Inventory - Raw Materials		
Inventory - Work-In-Progress		
Inventory -Finished Unsold Products		
Pre-Paid Expenses (insurance premiums, property taxes)		
TOTAL CURRENT ASSETS		
Non-Current Assets: Fixed		
Land and Buildings		
Machinery and Equipment		
Computers and Office Equipment, Furnishings		
Other		
TOTAL NON-CURRENT ASSETS		
TOTAL ASSETS		
Liabilities		
Current Liabilities: Short-Term Debts		
Accounts Payable		
Accrued Payroll		
Short Term Notes Due		
Current Portion of Long-Term Debt		
TOTAL CURRENT LIABILITIES		
Non-Current Liabilities: Long Term Debt		
Lease, Mortgage		
Long-Term Borrowings		
TOTAL NON-CURRENT LIABILITIES		
TOTAL LIABILITIES		

Figure 2.Sample Statement of Financial Activities - Revenue

REVENUE

Legend: FY2013 ACTUAL | FY2014 PROPOSED | FY2013 PRIOR YEAR

In Thousands: $1,580 | $1,600 | $1,620 | $1,640 | $1,660 | $1,680 | $1,700 | $1,720 | $1,740 | $1,760 | $1,780

REVENUE	FY2013 PRIOR YEAR	FY2014 PROPOSED	FY2013 ACTUAL	FY2013 VARIANCE	+/- PRIOR YEAR
Program 1	750000.00	760000.00	755000.00	(5000.00)	5000.00
Program 2	550000.00	560000.00	558000.00	(2000.00)	8000.00
Donations	300000.00	400000.00	340000.00	(60000.00)	40000.00
Grants	25000.00	25000.00	25000.00	0.00	0.00
Investment Interest	17000.00	17500.00	17100.00	(400.00)	100.00
TOTALS	$1,642,000.00	$1,762,500.00	$1,695,100.00	($67,400.00)	$0.00

Figure 3. Sample Statement of Financial Activities - Expenses

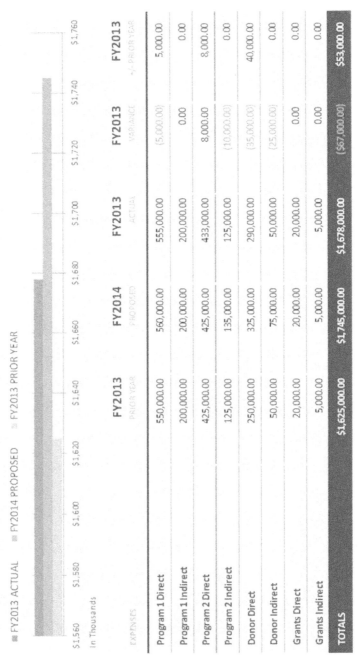

EXPENSES	FY2013 PRIOR YEAR	FY2014 PROPOSED	FY2013 ACTUAL	FY2013 VARIANCE	FY2013 +/- PRIOR YEAR
Program 1 Direct	550,000.00	560,000.00	555,000.00	(5,000.00)	5,000.00
Program 1 Indirect	200,000.00	200,000.00	200,000.00	0.00	0.00
Program 2 Direct	425,000.00	425,000.00	433,000.00	8,000.00	8,000.00
Program 2 Indirect	125,000.00	135,000.00	125,000.00	(10,000.00)	0.00
Donor Direct	250,000.00	325,000.00	290,000.00	(35,000.00)	40,000.00
Donor Indirect	50,000.00	75,000.00	50,000.00	(25,000.00)	0.00
Grants Direct	20,000.00	20,000.00	20,000.00	0.00	0.00
Grants Indirect	5,000.00	5,000.00	5,000.00	0.00	0.00
TOTALS	**$1,625,000.00**	**$1,745,000.00**	**$1,678,000.00**	**($67,000.00)**	**$53,000.00**

EXPENSES

■ FY2013 ACTUAL   ■ FY2014 PROPOSED   ■ FY2013 PRIOR YEAR

In Thousands

$1,560 $1,580 $1,600 $1,620 $1,640 $1,660 $1,680 $1,700 $1,720 $1,740 $1,760

Figure 4. Sample Statement of Financial Activities - Monthly

		Jan	Feb	Mar	Apl	May	Jun	Jul	Aug	Sep	Oct	Nov	Dec	YEARLY
Revenue	**TREND**													
Program 1		$ 1,086	$ 988	$ 920	$ 1,220	$ 890	$ 710	$ 1,210	$ 370	$ 540	$ 780	$ 920	$ 970	$ 10,604
Program 2		$ 1,500	$ 1,600	$ 1,980	$ 1,440	$ 1,500	$ 1,680	$ 1,550	$ 1,475	$ 1,370	$ 1,475	$ 1,500	$ 1,490	$ 18,560
Donor		$ 1,600	$ 1,200	$ 1,300	$ 1,208	$ 1,310	$ 700	$ 500	$ 490	$ 355	$ 410	$ 900	$ 870	$ 10,843
TOTAL REVENUE		$ 4,186	$ 3,788	$ 4,200	$ 3,868	$ 3,700	$ 3,090	$ 3,260	$ 2,335	$ 2,265	$ 2,665	$ 3,320	$ 3,330	$ 40,007
EXPENSES	**TREND**													
Program 1 Direct		$ 61	$ 78	$ 65	$ 29	$ 125	$ 49	$ 14	$ 26	$ 14	$ 129	$ 60	$ 65	$ 715
Program 1 Indirect		$ 1,000	$ 1,000	$ 1,000	$ 1,000	$ 1,000	$ 1,000	$ 1,000	$ 1,000	$ 1,000	$ 1,000	$ 1,000	$ 1,000	$ 12,000
Program 2 Direct		$ 99	$ 95	$ 51	$ 90	$ 21	$ 34	$ 30	$ 24	$ 109	$ 16	$ 21	$ 52	$ 642
Program 2 Indirect		$ 1,200	$ 1,200	$ 1,200	$ 1,200	$ 1,200	$ 1,200	$ 1,200	$ 1,200	$ 1,200	$ 1,200	$ 1,200	$ 1,200	$ 14,400
Donor Direct		$ 34	$ 78	$ 43	$ 30	$ 77	$ 54	$ 26	$ 13	$ 56	$ 30	$ 40	$ 63	$ 544
Donor Indirect		$ 500	$ 500	$ 500	$ 500	$ 500	$ 500	$ 500	$ 500	$ 500	$ 500	$ 500	$ 500	$ 6,000
TOTAL EXPENSES		$ 2,894	$ 2,951	$ 2,859	$ 2,849	$ 2,923	$ 2,837	$ 2,770	$ 2,763	$ 2,879	$ 2,875	$ 2,821	$ 2,880	$ 34,301
						#NAME?								
GROSS REVENUE		$ 1,292	$ 837	$ 1,341	$ 1,019	$ 777	$ 253	$ 490	$ (428)	$ (614)	$ (210)	$ 499	$ 450	$ 5,706

Figure 5. Sample Statement of Cash Flow

		2012
Cash Flows from Operating Activities		
Net Income	$	125,000.00
Adjustments		
Add back depreciation	$	7,500.00
Increase in accounts receivable	$	1,200.00
Decrease in prepaid expenses	$	(2,000.00)
Decrease in inventory	$	6,000.00
Increase in accounts payable	$	-
Net Cash provided by Operations	$	137,700.00
Cash Flow from Investing Activities		
Short-term Investments, net	$	115,000.00
Long-term Investment purchases	$	-
Proceeds from sale of Investments	$	-
Payments for property or equipment	$	12,000.00
Other	$	-
Cash Flow Investments	$	127,000.00
Cash Flow from Financing Activities		
Proceeds from notes payable	$	1,500.00
Proceed from contributions restricted		
for investment in endowment	$	55,000.00
Cash Flow Financing	$	56,500.00
NET INCREASE (DECREASE) IN CASH AND CASH EQUIVALENTS	$	192,300.00
CASH AND CASH EQUIVALENTS, BEGINNING OF YEAR	$	128,900.00
CASH AND CASH EQUIVALENTS, END OF YEAR	$	321,200.00

Figure 6. Sample Twelve Month Cash Flow

Twelve-Month Cash Flow

Nonprofit

Fiscal Year Begins: 7/1/2013

Cash Flow Summary

	Beginning	Jul-13	Aug-13	Sep-13	Oct-13	Nov-13	Dec-13	Jun-14	Monthly Average	Overview
Cash Summary										
Cash on Hand (beginning of month)	55,000	67,593	60,814	68,333	88,689	90,337			75,153	
Cash Available (on hand + receipts, before cash out)	67,593	76,065	89,850	103,626	109,061	100,919			95,904	
Cash Position (end of month)	67,593	60,814	68,333	88,689	90,337	84,141			78,463	
Cash Receipts										
Donors	5,616	3,889	24,411	31,642	14,647	3,034			15,525	
Program Revenue	4,498	3,493	1,987	1,029	2,911	4,234			2,731	
Grants	2,479	1,090	2,638	2,622	2,814	3,314			2,496	
Total Cash Receipts	12,593	8,472	29,036	35,293	20,372	10,582			8,646	
Cash Paid Out										
Purchases (specify)	521	323	274	451	104				335	
Gross wages (exact withdrawal)	10,572	14,514	10,561	13,170	12,478				12,259	
Supplies (office & oper.)	250	428	165	1,168	345				471	
Repairs & maintenance		2,200	163	67					486	
Rent	3,500	3,500	3,500	3,500	3,500				3,500	
Utilities	285	318	151	134	228				223	
Other (specify)	123	234	123	234	123				167	
Total Cash Paid Out	15,251	21,517	14,937	18,724	16,778				7,267	

Figure 7. Sample Statement of Departmental Expenses

	Budget FY 2012	Budget FY 2011	FY 2012 Actual	FY 2011 Actual	Variance
JOURNALS					
Revenue					
Single Issue Sales	$18,660	$20,603	$8,891	$10,477	($1,586)
Reprint / Rights Permission	$52,500	$113,667	$68,736	$64,437	$4,299
Online Subscriptions	$431,465	$257,164	$149,712	$119,430	$30,282
Subscriptions - Individual	$1,080,815	$1,182,772	$471,482	$627,061	($155,579)
Subscriptions - Students	$134,319	$152,781	$64,189	$81,030	($16,841)
Subscriptions - Institutional	$215,000	$448,550	$114,653	$237,336	($122,683)
Advertising Journal A	$28,000	$26,783	$7,845	$7,791	$54
Advertising Journal B	$3,232	$1,421	$720	$0	$720
Advertising Journal C	$157,000	$97,652	$57,210	$21,180	$36,030
Total Revenue	**$2,120,991**	**$2,301,393**	**$943,438**	**$1,168,742**	**($225,304)**
Expense Direct Product Cost					
Salary & Benefits	$237,973	$235,000	$145,306	$392,842	$247,536
Outside Editor	$116,000	$139,514	$45,000	$91,836	$46,836
Paper, Printer, Copier	$14,000	$402,916	$13,684	$151,096	$137,412
Postage / Shipping	$2,870	$151,304	$3,236	$96,776	$93,540
Production	$0	$19,986	$5,058	$6,959	$1,901
Outsourced Production Costs	$285,700	$0	$147,864	$0	($147,864)
Total Direct Product Cost	**$656,543**	**$948,720**	**$360,148**	**$739,509**	**$379,361**
Expense Indirect Product Cost					
Marketing	$191,342	$79,055	$101,371	$38,755	($62,616)
Administrative Operating	$142,100	$73,157	$43,749	$54,381	$10,632
Overhead Cost	$615,735	$788,571	$408,147	$456,804	$48,657
Total Indirect Product Cost	**$949,177**	**$940,783**	**$553,267**	**$549,940**	**($3,327)**
Total Expense	**$1,605,720**	**$1,889,503**	**$913,415**	**$1,289,449**	**$376,034**
TOTAL					
(Revenue - Expenses)	**$515,271**	**$411,890**	**$30,023**	**($120,707)**	**($150,730)**

Figure 8. Sample Modified Statement of Functional Expenses

EXPENSES	Program One	Program Two	Program Three	Research	Advocacy	Global	Administration	Development	Totals
Salaries	$ 1,100,000.00	$ 750,000.00	$ 2,000,000.00	$ 200,000.00	$ 200,000.00	$ 250,000.00	$ 250,000.00	$ 250,000.00	$ 5,000,000.00
Benefits	$ 275,000.00	$ 187,500.00	$ 500,000.00	$ 50,000.00	$ 50,000.00	$ 62,500.00	$ 62,500.00	$ 62,500.00	$ 1,250,000.00
Payroll Taxes	$ 91,300.00	$ 62,250.00	$ 166,000.00	$ 16,600.00	$ 16,600.00	$ 20,750.00	$ 20,750.00	$ 20,750.00	$ 394,250.00
Contracted Services	$ 85,000.00	$ 450,000.00	$ 850,000.00	$ 5,000.00	$ 10,000.00	$ 25,000.00	$ 270,000.00	$ 15,000.00	$ 1,710,000.00
Information Technology	$ 150,000.00	$ 75,000.00	$ 200,000.00	$ 10,000.00	$ 50,000.00	$ 25,000.00	$ 150,000.00	$ 10,000.00	$ 670,000.00
Utilities	$ 15,000.00	$ 35,000.00	$ 15,000.00	$ 15,000.00	$ 15,000.00	$ 15,000.00	$ 15,000.00	$ 15,000.00	$ 140,000.00
Insurance	$ -	$ -	$ -	$ -	$ -	$ -	$ 5,000.00	$ -	$ 5,000.00
Postage	$ 150,000.00	$ 15,000.00	$ 250,000.00	$ 3,000.00	$ 10,000.00	$ 10,000.00	$ 18,000.00	$ 15,000.00	$ 471,000.00
Office Supplies	$ 1,000.00	$ 1,000.00	$ 3,000.00	$ 1,000.00	$ 1,000.00	$ 1,000.00	$ 25,000.00	$ 1,000.00	$ 34,000.00
Cost of Goods Sold	$ 75,000.00	$ 25,000.00	$ 400,000.00	$ -	$ -	$ -	$ -	$ 5,000.00	$ 505,000.00
Occupancy	$ 72,500.00	$ 72,500.00	$ 72,500.00	$ 72,500.00	$ 72,500.00	$ 72,500.00	$ 72,500.00	$ 72,500.00	$ 580,000.00
Depreciation	$ 100,000.00	$ 100,000.00	$ 260,000.00	$ -	$ -	$ -	$ 100,000.00	$ -	$ 560,000.00
Accounting	$ -	$ -	$ -	$ -	$ -	$ -	$ 30,000.00	$ -	$ 30,000.00
Legal Fees	$ -	$ -	$ -	$ -	$ -	$ -	$ 50,000.00	$ -	$ 50,000.00
Travel	$ 5,000.00	$ 80,000.00	$ 15,000.00	$ 5,000.00	$ 10,000.00	$ 85,000.00	$ 160,000.00	$ 20,000.00	$ 380,000.00
Investment Management Fees	$ -	$ -	$ -	$ -	$ -	$ -	$ 25,000.00	$ -	$ 380,000.00
Royalties	$ -	$ -	$ 80,000.00	$ -	$ -	$ -	$ -	$ -	$ 80,000.00
Professional Membership Fees	$ 250.00	$ 250.00	$ 500.00	$ 500.00	$ 200.00	$ 150.00	$ 500.00	$ 300.00	$ 2,650.00
Staff Development	$ -	$ 250.00	$ -	$ -	$ -	$ -	$ 50,000.00	$ -	$ 50,000.00
Marketing	$ 750,000.00	$ 250,000.00	$ 350,000.00	$ -	$ 5,000.00	$ 5,000.00	$ -	$ 10,000.00	$ 1,370,000.00
Totals	**$ 2,870,050.00**	**$ 2,083,500.00**	**$ 5,182,000.00**	**$ 378,600.00**	**$ 440,300.00**	**$ 571,900.00**	**$ 1,304,250.00**	**$ 497,050.00**	**$ 13,661,900.00**

Section II: Strategic Planning

"Planning is bringing the future into the present so that you can do something about it now." - Alan Lakein

CHAPTER FOUR

Defining the Now

Planning for the future can be one of the most frustrating things organizations, and its employees, encounter during its tenure of service. The very words can strike fear, panic, and anxiety into the hearts of workers – and managers. And for good reason. Planning takes time, patience; courageous leadership; an honest look at organizational programs and results; advocates change; and many times, a shifting of organizational resources. Many employees wonder if the new strategy will eliminate their jobs. Others view planning as nothing more than an exercise to create an impressive archival, but useless, record for the board. For most organizations, planning for the future involves the hiring of consultants who tell you what you must do if your organization is to become more meaningful. Many consultants pour much time, energy, and effort into guiding your organization along a transformational path. And for the most part, they do good work and leave you with a doable strategy for the future. But the real challenge lies in what transpires after the consultants have gone. It is very easy for the leadership to take a passive role in the planning while the consultants are involved, after all, the consultants are well paid for their work. But when the consultants go, it may be difficult for the leadership to insert themselves into the driver's seat of a project that was directed by others. In all honesty, generating the kind of commitment needed to implement a new strategy into a full-fledged operational stage will be difficult for the dormant leader. Knowing what you want to do and where you want to be is quite different from performing the actions that are required to take you to the Promised Land. Intentions and desire may be good, but picking up on work begun by others can be daunting. This is where many strategies meet their doom and become documents that sit on a shelf and gather dust. But there is another way.

This chapter is offered as an alternative way of strategic planning for those leaders who wish to roll up their sleeves and lead their organization on a journey that will strengthen their organization, employees, and services to the client community. This section of *The Holy Grail of Managing a Nonprofit* was designed as a practical tool that any leader can use to conduct and implement meaningful planning for the future.

Begin by Defining Your Current Situation

In this section, we will help you:

- Identify and Convene a Core Strategic Planning Team
- Examine & describe current business / operating model and presumed strategy
- Engage stakeholders (client community, board, funders) to collect input from their perspective of the organization
- Identify your competition
- Examine other organizations with similar missions but alternative approaches to solving the mission problem

Identify and Convene Core Strategy Team

Begin your planning journey by creating a Core Strategy Team. Not only must the CEO be a member of this team, as his/her commitment to the process is essential for overall success, the CEO must be the chief spokesperson and head cheerleader of the process. Planning for the future works best when the CEO is seen as deeply committed to the future path of the organization. In fact, many management experts would argue that strategy is the main and most important function of a CEO.

The Strategy Team should:

- Consist of 6 to 10 members. Include the CEO, CFO, key functional leaders, and credible representatives from the front lines.
- Assign a team leader – does not have to be CEO (The team leader coordinates and schedules planning activities but is not assigned more power or veto rights. The group will need to decide how difficult decisions will be made.))
- Meet 2 to 4 hours weekly (best results); 2 to 4 hours every other week (minimum)
- Consider these meetings as part of their responsibility to improve operations and deliver on mission
- Engage in serious debate throughout the journey – discussions are the foundations of the process
- Commit from 4 to 6 months on this future creating process (depending on the size and scope of your operation)
- Try to avoid looking in the rear view mirror (the past) and focus on the horizon; on aspirations of an ideal future
- Make time throughout the process to update staff of findings
- Bring in staff experts to assist with discussions in their work related area
- If at any time during the process you expose new and unexpected insights that lead you back to a previous step, go back and revisit that step and plug in the new found knowledge

Examine & Describe Current Business Model and Operations Strategy

Ophthalmologists suggest that individual's under the age of 40 with no family history of eye disease should receive a comprehensive eye exam every three years. The ophthalmologist typically asks questions about any general health and vision related issues you may be experiencing. A host of visual screenings will be performed to measure total eye health. The main reason for these screenings is to identify and treat potential risks of future-related problems, such as cataracts, glaucoma, or some other eye condition. For the journey you are about to embark upon, consider yourself the ophthalmologist and your organization the patient. Ask as many questions about organizational health as you can while keeping in mind that your goal is to provide a treatment that will preserve optimal organizational health well into the future. Let's begin the examination.

What does your portfolio of services/programs look like? Use **Table 1 through Table 7** as a templates to inventory programs and services. It is important that you show both expenses (includes direct & indirect costs) and gross revenue for all programs.

How does your portfolio compare against your mission and vision statements?

Organizational Exercise 6	CHALLENGE: Develop a checklist showing match or mismatch of services. (Ask: Do our programs still fit the mission / vision. If you did not have this program, would we develop one today?

Table 1 Program Inventory

PROGRAM & SERVICES INVENTORY.			
Department Providing Service	**Program Name**	**Program Expense**	**Program Revenue**

Table 2 Portfolio Mission / Vision Checklist

Rate each program/service you offer against both mission and vision. See scale below for number criteria. Current Mission Statement: Current Vision Statement:		
Program Name	**Mission**	**Vision**
Program A – brief description		
Program B – brief description		
Program C – brief description		
Rating Scale: 1. No relevance 2. Historical relevance only 3. Moderate relevance 4. High relevance 5. Absolute, unequivocal relevance		

Table 3 Program Mission Gap Template

Current Mission:		
Programs That Address Mission	**What Program Actually Does**	**What Program Should Do**

Table 4 Vision Gap Template

Current Vision:		
Programs That Address Vision	**What Program Actually Does**	**What Program Should Do**

Program Problem Gap Template

Using information gathered from the Program Mission Gap and Program Vision Gap templates, list programs that have significant gaps between the desired and actual outcomes. State the gap impact on each of the listed organization categories. (Gap impact should be expressed in negative terms. Use one template for each program.)

Table 5 Identify Gap Problem

Name of Program: Identified Gap Problem:		
	What Program Actually Does	**What it Should Do**
Reputation Impact		
Process Impact		
HR Impact		
Budget Impact		

Table 6 Identify Different Types of Clients

Who are your current and potential clients? List the different types of clients
- Where is the demand for your programs coming from?
- Are you serving the clients you intended to serve?
- Identify client segments.

Client Segment	# of client	# of possible clients	# of Target Clients	Revenue from Segment	Cost per Segment	Annual Renewal or Repeat Rate per Segment
Web visits						
Conference Goers						
Membership Dues						
Program A						
Program B						
Program C						
TOTAL						

Table 6.1 Analysis of Client Data

1. Which of your programs are in the biggest demand?

    _____

    _____

    _____

    _____

    _____

2. Which of your programs are serving the clients you intended to serve? Which are not?

    _____

    _____

    _____

    _____

    _____

3. Are you allocating too many resources to what you know how to do instead of what you should be doing?

    _____

    _____

    _____

Table 7Business Model Template

What does your presumed business model look like? (By business model we mean: How do you make money for your organization and deliver on mission? Who pays? How much? How often? Questions to ask:

- Stable source of revenue?
- Expenses not outpacing revenue?
- Self-sufficient?
- Do all staff know how your nonprofit generates revenue?

Revenue Generating Programs	Pricing (How much per client)	Who Pays for Use of Program (be specific); list all sources of funding	Frequency of Payment Annually? Quarterly? Monthly?	Profit Margin Use data from Table 1 to calculate: PR-PE = P $\frac{P}{PR}$ = PM

<u>Legend</u>

PR = Program Revenue   **P** = Profit

PE = Program Expense   **PM** = Profit Margin

How does your business model help or hinder attraction of new clients?

- List the processes used to deliver each product or service. Use **Table 8** - Process Audit Template. Pay attention to:

  - ✓ Is it cost effective?
  - ✓ Does your client community value the product/service?
  - ✓ What do your measurable results tell you?

Product Name

Table 8 Process Audit

People Involved	Staff (total FTE): Volunteers (total number): Vendors(list all):
Materials Used	Do you regularly seek bids /quotes? What is organization policy on bids/quotes? Adequate quality?
Equipment Used	Satisfactory? Outdated?
Standards Used	Industry standards? Organization created standards?
Procedures Used	Describe how product or service is created from scratch through delivery to client community:
Identified Problems	Describe problems (and cause) associated with the process:
Impact Problems	Which problems have a significant impact on: • Profitability • Time lost • Client Community. • Morale • Organization Reputation

What capabilities does your organization currently possess? Lack? Can be built upon?

Capabilities are the internal abilities and expertise used for meeting client community needs. They include:

- Human resources
- Governance resources
- Financial resources
- Information resources
- Geographic resources
- Other specialized resources

Use Capabilities Audit **Table 9** to conduct an audit.

Capabilities Audit

How to Use Table 9

Answer the questions in Table 9 using the following Ratings. (Please note that you will undoubtedly uncover other questions to be asked as you go through this exercise. Ask those questions and rate them. You may also want to add different capabilities to audit. Additionally, it is a good idea to keep notes as you go through this exercise. You want to capture as much data as you can about your organization's abilities – or lack of - to deliver mission to the client community.) To gather this data you may choose to survey staff only; staff & board only; staff, board, and client community

Table 9 Rating Scale	
How Effective	Improvement Priority
1 = Needs Significant Help	1 = Highest priority
2 = Minimal Acceptance; help still needed	2 = Moderate Priority
3 = Good Enough	3 = If No Other Priorities Exist
4 = Great	4 = Leave Alone

Table 9 Capabilities Audit

Capabilities	Questions	How Effective	Improvement Priority
Collaboration	Does your staff work well together across departmental boundaries to achieve organizational goals? Does your organization show signs of departmental silos?		
Culture	Do you have a culture that respects staff, clients, vendors, & board? Do you have a written set of core values?		
Efficiency	Are you producing products and services at lowest cost? Are you purchasing supplies at the best rates?		
Geographic Resources	Are there unique resources available to your organization based on location?		
Governance Resources	Do you have a knowledgeable board? Do you have a diverse board – from all walks & careers? Does the board understand its role vs the role of staff? Do board policies reflect the nature of the organization's mission & work?		
Human Resources	Does staff have the training and competence to move the organization forward at a high level of quality? Does your organization have up-to-date human resources policies?		
Financial Resources	Does the organization have a stable and consistent source of revenue? Does the organization have an investment portfolio? Does the investment portfolio have enough assets to cover 6 months of operating expenses? Does your organization get an annual financial audit?		
Information Resources	How well does your organization distribute information to clients? How well does your organization collect, sort, & use data for decision making?		
Client Connected	Does your organization have long lasting relationships with the client community? Do you members trust you at the highest levels?		

What capabilities does your organization currently possess? Lack? Can be built upon?

Use the results from the Capabilities Audit (Table 9) identify capabilities using **Table 10**:

- Which capabilities are weak but should be built out?
- Which capabilities are weak and can stay weak or be eliminated?
- What are your strengths?
- Do your strengths have a direct impact on client value?
- Are you spreading yourself too thin?
- List capabilities you wish your organization had but does not.

Table 10 Capabilities Summary

Capabilities that Have Most Impact on Client Community	Our Strongest Capabilities (list in rank order)	Weak Capabilities Worth Building Out	Capabilities Wish List
1	1	1	1
2	2	2	2
3	3	3	3

Are there other competencies, capacities, or advantages not yet identified that your organization possesses? List them in **Table 11**.

Examples might include:

- Organization is quick to adapt to changing trends, landscape, etc.
- Organization is made up of highly skilled employees.
- Leading experts are part of the client community

Table 11 Other Competencies, Capabilities, or Advantages

Other Competencies	Other Capabilities	Other Advantages

Based on what you currently know about your business model and operations strategy, what do you think makes your nonprofit attractive to the client community? What are the results that only your nonprofit can get? Use **Tables 12 a & b** than complete **Table 13** exercise.

Table 12A Attractive to Clients

List the top three things about your nonprofit **YOU** think are attractive to your client community

1._____

_____

2._____

_____

3._____

_____

Table 12B Unique Results

List the top three results that only your nonprofit can achieve (it would be difficult or impossible for your competitors to imitate programs that produce results like yours.)

1._____

_____

2._____

_____

3._____

_____

Table 13Hole in Universe

If your organization disappeared over night, what hole would be left in the universe?

Real debate and dialogue is needed here. If your organization went out of business today, what would the hole in the universe for your client community look like? Would there be a hole? Can they get all that you offer somewhere else? **Make a list of the services or programs that your client community** could not get some place else if your organization closed its doors forever.

_____

_____

_____

_____

_____

_____

_____

_____

_____

_____

_____

Engage Stakeholders (Client Community, Board, Funders) To Collect Input from Their Perspective of the Organization

Now that you have collected data and insights from your core strategy team, it is time to gather the perspectives of shareholders not participating on the core team. Start with functional area staff (who are not on core team), ask & record answers to:

- What is the current business & mission strategy?
- What are the most significant issues facing the nonprofit?
- Where is the organization's strength? Weakness?
- What opportunities look promising?

See **Table 14** for examples of Employee Survey

Table 14 Employee Survey

What three things does our organization do well?	
What three things need to be improved?	
How do we make money to support programs and pay for staff?	
What is our mission?	
Name all of the ways we deliver on mission.	
Which client community needs are we satisfying?	
Which client community needs are we missing?	
What are the biggest problems facing the organization?	
What is our strategic direction?	
Is there a part of the client community that we could be serving, but we are not?	
Are there things we are doing that we should stop doing?	
Are there things we are not doing that we should be doing?	
What things are we doing that we should continue doing?	

Now, survey the client community, board members, and vendors. What does the outside world see? Questions should invite comment:

- On nonprofit's past accomplishments
- Its reputation
- The relevance of its model for the future
- Its capabilities. to deliver on mission
- Its potential for long-term sustainability

Tables 15, 16, & 17 contain examples of Client Survey, Board Survey, and Vendor Survey

Table 15 Client Community Survey

What three things does our organization do well to help you?	
What three things need to be improved?	
Does our organization have a good reputation in the world you live in?	
Are we meeting all of your current needs? If not, what are we missing?	
What do anticipate your future needs to be?	
Is this organization prepared to meet those future needs?	
If you could add one thing to our portfolio of services, what would it be?	
What are the biggest problems facing the organization?	
What are some of the current trends that may have a negative impact on your life?	
What other organizations do you turn to for support or information?	
Are there things we are doing that we should stop doing?	
Are there things we are not doing that we should be doing?	
What things are we doing that we should continue doing?	

Table 16 Board Survey

What three things does our organization do well?	
What three things need to be improved?	
Does our organization have a good reputation in the world you live in?	
Are we meeting all of client community needs? If not, what are we missing?	
What do anticipate client community future needs to be?	
Is this organization prepared to meet those future needs?	
If you could add one thing to our portfolio of services, what would it be?	
What are the biggest problems facing the organization?	
What are some of the current trends that may have a negative impact on our client community?	
What other organizations do our client community turn to for support or information?	
Are there things we are doing that we should stop doing?	
Are there things we are not doing that we should be doing?	
What things are we doing that we should continue doing?	

Table 17 Vendor Survey

What three things does our organization do well?	
What three things need to be improved?	
Does our organization have a good reputation in the world you live in?	
What industry or market trends should we be aware of?	
From your perspective, what does this organization need to do to prepare to meet those future trends?	
Who do you consider our competitors to be?	
How do we compare with those competitors – our services, culture, results, & pricing?	
What is the biggest issue, when dealing with us that we should address?	
If you could add one thing to our portfolio of services, what would it be?	
What are other organizations doing successfully that we should consider?	
Are there things we are doing that we should stop doing?	
Are there things we are not doing that we should be doing?	
What things are we doing that we should continue doing?	

Perform a Google search. for your organization. Record answers to questions on Google Search Template on **Table 18.**

Note the number of times organization appears in

- search
- newspapers
- professional trade journal/magazine
- press releases
- social problem research
- social problem innovation

Table 18 Google Search

1. How many times does your organization appear in the search?	
2. How many times is your organization mentioned in newspapers?	
3. How many times is your organization covered by a professional trade journal/magazine in your field of operation?	
4. How many press releases did you uncover?	
5. Is your media coverage sporadic and in outlets visited or read by your targeted audience?	
Perform a Google Search on the social problems your organization exists to solve	
6. When research is cited on this problem, how often is your organization mentioned?	
7. When innovative approaches are cited on this problem, how often is your organization mentioned?	
8. When positive results for solving the problem are cited, how often is your organization mentioned?	
9. When terminology or buzz words related to the social problem are Googled, how often is your organization mentioned?	
10. How often is your organization mentioned in social media: Facebook, Twitter, blogs, etc.?	

It is now time to analyze the data you have collected. You will need the following tables with their data.

> - 1, 2, 7, 10
> - 5
> - 6
> - 8, 9, 11
> - 12, 15, 16, 17
> - 13
> - 18

Compare data collected on **Tables 1, 2, 7, 10**

Table 19 Summary Chart I

Program Name			
Program Expense			
Program Revenue			
Who Pays			
PM			
MR			
VR			
Impact Capabilities			
Wish Capabilities			

Table Legend

Program Expense: from Table 1, column 3

MR = Mission Rating: from Table 2, column 2

Program Revenue: from Table 1, column 4

VR = Vision Rating: from Table 2, column 3

Who Pays: from Table 7, column 3

Impact Capabilities associated with program: from Table 10, Column 1

PM = Profit Margin: from Table 7, column 5

Table 20 Summary Chart II

Organizational Capacity
Compare data collected on Tables 8, 9, 11

Staff	R	Procedures	R	Strongest Org Capabilities	Biggest Org Impact Problems
Training (T9, r7)		Industry Standards (T8,r4)		1.	1.
Collaboration (T9,r2)		Efficiency (T9, r4)			
Culture (T9, r3)		Equipment (T8, r3)		2.	2.
Competent (T9, r7)		Materials (T8, r2)			
HR Policies		Information (T9, r9)		3.	3.
FTE (T8, r1)		Financial			

Legend	
T = Table	**R** = Rating Number with number
r = Row on table	1. needs significant help
	2. minimal acceptance; help still needed
	3. good enough
	4. great

Table 21 Summary Chart III.a

Compare Data from Tables (12, 15, 16, & 17)	
What three things does the nonprofit do well to help the client community?	Core Strategic Planning Team. Responses (from Table 12) 1. 2. 3. Employee Survey 1. 2. 3. Client Community Survey 1. 2. 3. Board Survey 1. 2. 3. Vendor Survey 1. 2. 3.

Table 22 Summary Chart III.b

What three things need to be improved?	Employee Survey 1. 2. 3. Client Community Survey 1. 2. 3. Board Survey 1. 2. 3. Vendor Survey 1. 2. 3.

Table 23 Summary Chart III.c

Does our organization have a good reputation in the world you live in?	Client Community Survey 1. 2. 3. Board Survey 1. 2. 3. Vendor Survey 1. 2. 3.

Table 24 Summary Chart III.d

Are we meeting all of the client community needs? If not, what are we missing?	Client Community Survey (list missing) 1. 2. 3. Board Survey (List missing) 1. 2. 3. Employee Survey (Question # 7) 1. 2. 3.

Table 25 Summary Chart III.e

What do anticipate future client community needs to be?	Client Community Survey 1. 2. 3. Board Survey 1. 2. 3.

Table 26 Summary Chart III.f

Is this organization prepared to meet those future needs?	Client Community Survey 1. 2. 3. Board Survey 1. 2. 3.

Table 27 Summary Chart III.g

If you could add one thing to our portfolio of services, what would it be?	Client Community Survey 1. 2. 3. Board Survey 1. 2. 3. Vendor Survey (Question #9) 1. 2. 3.

Table 28 Summary Chart III.h

What are the biggest problems facing the organization?	Client Community Survey 1. 2. 3. Board Survey 1. 2. 3. Employee Survey (Question #8) 1. 2. 3.

Table 29 Summary Chart III.i

What are some of the current trends that may have a negative impact on the client community?	Client Community Survey 1. 2. 3. Board Survey 1, 2. 3. Vendor Survey (Question # 4) 1. 2. 3.

Table 30 Summary Chart III.j

What other organizations does the client community turn to for support or information?	Client Community Survey 1. 2. 3. Board Survey 1. 2. 3. Vendor Survey (Question # 10) 1. 2. 3.

Table 31 Summary Chart III.k

Are there things we are doing that we should stop doing?	Employee Survey 1. 2. 3. Client Community Survey 1. 2. 3. Board Survey 1. 2. 3. Vendor Survey 1. 2. 3.

Table 32 Summary Chart III.l

Are there things we are not doing that we should be doing?	Employee Survey 1. 2. 3. Client Community Survey 1. 2. 3. Board Survey 1. 2. 3. Vendor Survey 1. 2. 3.

Table 33 Summary Chart III.m

What things are we doing that we should continue doing?	Employee Survey 1. 2. 3. Client Community Survey 1. 2. 3. Board Survey 1. 2. 3. Vendor Survey 1. 2. 3.

Table 34 Summary Chart IV – Hole in Universe

Re-examine your list from the exercise found on **Table 13**. From all that you have learned conducting this strategic plan so far, does the list still seem relevant and accurate? If necessary make changes and label new document <u>Summary Chart IV</u>

_____

_____

_____

_____

_____

_____

_____

_____

_____

_____

_____

_____

_____

Table 35 Summary Chart V Google Analysis

Examine the responses in Table 18 Instructions: Circle Yes or No	
Is your organization's story being told in the broader media?	Yes No
Are your getting significant coverage in the outlets that reach your client and potential client community?	Yes No
Are you getting the needle moving coverage to broaden the awareness about your organization's work?	Yes No
Does your organization suffer from a lack of organizational messages?	Yes No
Do you issue press releases? If so, do they make to the major media outlets?	Yes No Yes No
Does your organization have an identifiable spokesperson?	Yes No
Is most of the media coverage about the societal problem your organization is trying to solve rather than about your organization and its results?	Yes No
Is anyone from your organization writing op-editorial articles for the major media outlets?	Yes No
Does your organization appear to lack a focused public relations campaign?	Yes No

This would be a good time to convene key staff who are not members of the Core Strategy Team to review findings. It is not only important to share what you have done but to listen to the questions and suggestions of key employees. These discussions can only improve the formulation of the future strategy. This meeting will also serve as a way to begin the process of employee commitment to a new strategy.

Identify Your Competition

Yes, your nonprofit does have competition. Understanding the growing number of participants in your field is important to your future.

- During this phase of planning we will help you to list others in your field, the programs they offer, who they offer services to, and how they offer them to clients
- For each listed competitor, we will help you to show how your nonprofit is different
- You will want to uncover your program areas that are particularly crowded with other participants
- You will want to uncover program areas where other participants have not yet filled
- You will want to examine and understand the external stresses pressing against your client and potential client community
  - ➢ Does your organization help your client community overcome these stresses?

Competition may come in the following forms:

- Internet / Social media
  - ➢ Access to Information
- Other nonprofits in your field
  - ➢ Competing for your donors for funding
  - ➢ May provide similar or same services
- Corporate foundations
  - ➢ May offer similar programs
- Private foundations
  - ➢ Same as corporate foundations
- Government
  - ➢ Limited funds to award
- Client community external pressures

Competition from the Internet and Social Media

Information – Let's face it, in this day and age of social media many words, rumors, thoughts, and musings are passed off as information. Therefore, it is important that you know as many of the sources from where your client community gets information. If you expect to be the go-to expert in your field, you will need to provide the highest quality information in a timely manner in order to win your clients complete trust and loyalty. Otherwise, your clients will turn to others sources for information and will be less committed to supporting your organization.

Competition from Other Nonprofits in Your Field

You must be aware of other nonprofits in your field as:

- Some provide the same or similar services as your organization
- Some compete for dollars from your client community
- Some compete for the grant money you want
- Some compete for your staff

It is important that you discover and understand how other nonprofits compete with you.

Corporate Foundations

As corporate social responsibility outreach programs increase, you must be aware of the potential CSR impact on your organization.

- Corporations target nonprofit staff to fill their talent pool
- CSR programs may target your field as the area they wish to engage
- CSR programs may be receiving the same corporate funding that previously was awarded to nonprofits as grants or sponsorships.

Competition from Private Foundations

You should be aware of the growing number of private foundations, approximately 86,000 plus in the U.S.A.

- Some of these foundations will be in your field and provide funding for programs that match their interests.
- Knowing how and who they have funded in your field would be beneficial to your future plans or partnership.

Competition from Government

As the U.S. national debt continues to spiral upward, both the federal and state governments are re-examining how and where they spend funds intended for social issues. Grants that subsidized your organization in the past may be reduced or eliminated in the future. Politicians and government agencies are competing fiercely over discretionary funds. New rules and regulations may also make it difficult for you to compete for government funds. If your organization has significant reliance on government grants and funds, you will need to stay current on all pending legislation and regulations that apply to your field. The government will no longer give you money just because your organization exists. You will need to demonstrate your efforts are making a difference – a difference that no one else can make.

Competition from External Pressures on Client Community

There are other people, organizations and sources of information that are also competing for your client community time. Some are benign, others are overtly seeking your client community. Family, friends, media, and work – all influence your clients to some extent. For your organization's success, it is important that you know and understand the life circumstances of your client community. What generation are they from? What do they believe in? What do they value? The more you understand about these pressures the better you will be able to serve your client community.

Use **Tables 36 and 37** to identify your competition.

Instructions: Research the five categories listed under competitors against your programs.

Table 36 Competitive Landscape Framework

Competitors	Program 1	Program 2	Program 3	Program 4
Internet/Social Media List possible ways your clients can get information from Internet or social media for each program (note: validly of information)				
Nonprofits List nonprofits in your field for each program				
Corporate Foundations List corporate foundations that support programs similar to yours for each program				
Private Foundations List private foundations that support programs similar to yours for each program				
Government List federal & state grantors in your field for each program				

For each program from your Competitive Landscape Framework, plot competitors on the grid below to get a visual of the number of direct competitors. Compare the competitor's work, product, or service against the work you do.

Table 37 Competitive Landscape Map

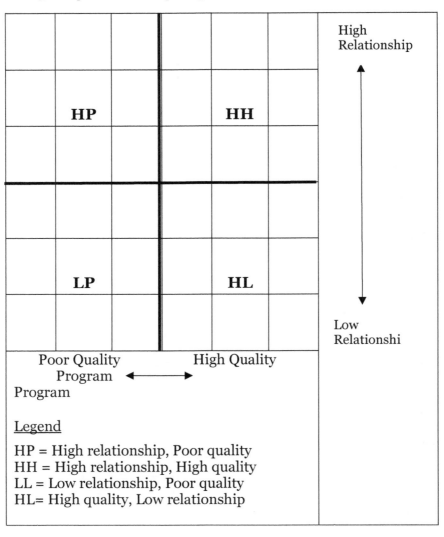

	High Relationship
HP	HH
LP	HL
	Low Relationshi

Poor Quality Program ←——→ High Quality Program
Program

Legend

HP = High relationship, Poor quality
HH = High relationship, High quality
LL = Low relationship, Poor quality
HL= High quality, Low relationship

Other Organizations with Similar Missions

Examine other organizations with similar missions but not the same as yours. You are interested in learning alternative approaches to solving the mission problem. This exercise will help you examine how different types of participants approach the delivery of solutions to social problems. What to look for:

- What are their strengths?
- What are their weaknesses?
- What is their success rate?
- Potential partners?

As you examine each alternative way used by other organizations trying to solve the same problem you are trying to solve, you will want to

(a.) Describe the business model used
(b.) Identify strategy for solving societal problem
(c.) Discuss the pros and cons of the alternative way
(d.) Discuss key takeaway for your organization

To answer these questions, select three organizations that deliver services similar to your organization but in a different field. You will want to use the following charts to collect data from their websites and Federal IRS Form 990. If the organization does not post the 990, you can find it on Guidestar.com. All you need to create a free client account on Guidestar is your email address and a password. Although most of the information relevant to the following forms can be found on Part I, page1 of the 990, it is highly suggested that you explore the entire form, especially

- Statements of Service Accomplishments
- Statement of Revenue
- Statement of Functional Expenses

- Balance Sheet
- Compensation of Officers, Directors, Trustees
- Supplemental Information Schedule O

Figure 9 Federal 990 Form

Table 38 Alternative Provider #1with Similar Mission Template

1	Name of Organization	
2	Apparent Strategy for Solving Problem	
3	How do They Measure Success (Website)	
4	Who Pays for Use of Program (Website & 990) (be as specific as you can – list all sources of funding)	
5	Frequency of Payment (Website) (annual. quarterly, monthly, per use)	
6	Total Employees (Part I, q5, 990)	
7	Total Volunteers (Part I,q6, 990)	
8	Total Revenue (Part VIII, q12, 990)	
9	Total Expenses (Part IX, q25, 990)	
10	Total Cash on Hand (Part X, q1, 990)	
11	Total Assets (Part X, q16, 990)	
12	Total Liabilities (Part X, q26, 990)	
13	Total Investment Income (Part VIII q3, 990)	
14	Revenue from Largest Program (Part III, q4a, 990)	
15	Expense from Largest Program (Part III, q4a, 990)	
16	Revenue from 2nd Largest Program (Part III, q4b, 990)	
17	Expenses from 2nd Largest Program (Part III, q4b, 990)	
18	Revenue from 3rd Largest Program Part III, q4c, 990)	
19	Expenses from 3rd Largest Program (Part III, q4c, 990)	
20	Grants / Contributions Received (Part VIII, q1f, 990)	
21	Fundraising Revenue (Part VIII, q8a, 990)	
22	Apparent Strengths	
23	Apparent Weaknesses	

Table 39Findings from table 38

What did you discover about the organization's: (Data recorded on Table 38)	
Resources • Financial • Human • Physical • Technical	
Capabilities • Methods • Networks	
Core Competencies • Expert knowledge • Service delivery speed • Locations	
Strategy	
Reputation	
Can you identify the biggest strength of organization	
Can you identify the biggest weakness of organization	
How do they create value for their client community	

Table 40 Alternative Provider #2 with Similar Mission Template

1	Name of Organization	
2	Apparent Strategy for Solving Problem	
3	How do They Measure Success (Website)	
4	Who Pays for Use of Program (Website & 990(be as specific as you can – list all sources of funding)	
5	Frequency of Payment (Website) (annual. quarterly, monthly, per use)	
6	Total Employees (Part I, q5, 990)	
7	Total Volunteers (Part I,q6, 990)	
8	Total Revenue (Part VIII, q12, 990)	
9	Total Expenses (Part IX, q25, 990)	
10	Total Cash on Hand (Part X, q1, 990)	
11	Total Assets (Part X, q16, 990)	
12	Total Liabilities (Part X, q26, 990)	
13	Total Investment Income (Part VIII q3, 990)	
14	Revenue from Largest Program (Part III, q4a, 990)	
15	Expense from Largest Program (Part III, q4a, 990)	
16	Revenue from 2nd Largest Program (Part III, q4b, 990)	
17	Expenses from 2nd Largest Program (Part III, q4b, 990)	
18	Revenue from 3rd Largest Program Part III, q4c, 990)	
19	Expenses from 3rd Largest Program (Part III, q4c, 990)	
20	Grants / Contributions Received (Part VIII, q1f, 990)	
21	Fundraising Revenue (Part VIII, q8a, 990)	
22	Apparent Strengths	
23	Apparent Weaknesses	

Table 41Findings from Table 40

What did you discover about the organization's: (Data recorded on Table 40)	
Resources • Financial • Human • Physical • Technical	
Capabilities • Methods • Networks	
Core Competencies • Expert knowledge • Service delivery speed • Locations	
Strategy	
Reputation	
Can you identify the biggest strength of organization	
Can you identify the biggest weakness of organization	
How do they create value for their client community	

Table 42 Alternative Provider #3 with Similar Mission Template

1	Name of Organization	
2	Apparent Strategy for Solving Problem	
3	How do They Measure Success (Website)	
4	Who Pays for Use of Program (Website & 990) (be as specific as you can – list all sources of funding)	
5	Frequency of Payment (Website) (annual. quarterly, monthly, per use)	
6	Total Employees (Part I, q5, 990)	
7	Total Volunteers (Part I,q6, 990)	
8	Total Revenue (Part VIII, q12, 990)	
9	Total Expenses (Part IX, q25, 990)	
10	Total Cash on Hand (Part X, q1, 990)	
11	Total Assets (Part X, q16, 990)	
12	Total Liabilities (Part X, q26, 990)	
13	Total Investment Income (Part VIII q3, 990)	
14	Revenue from Largest Program (Part III, q4a, 990)	
15	Expense from Largest Program (Part III, q4a, 990)	
16	Revenue from 2nd Largest Program (Part III, q4b, 990)	
17	Expenses from 2nd Largest Program (Part III, q4b, 990)	
18	Revenue from 3rd Largest Program Part III, q4c, 990)	
19	Expenses from 3rd Largest Program (Part III, q4c, 990)	
20	Grants / Contributions Received (Part VIII, q1f, 990)	
21	Fundraising Revenue (Part VIII, q8a, 990)	
22	Apparent Strengths	
23	Apparent Weaknesses	

Table 43 Findings from table 42

What did you discover about the organization's: (Data recorded on Table 42)	

Resources
 	
  • Financial
  • Human
  • Physical
  • Technical	

·Capabilities
 	
  • Methods
  • Networks	

Core Competencies
 	
  • Expert knowledge
  • Service delivery speed
  • Locations	

Strategy	
Reputation	
Can you identify the biggest strength of organization	
Can you identify the biggest weakness of organization	
How do they create value for their client community	

This would be a good time to convene key staff who are not members of the Core Strategy Team to review findings. It is not only important to share what you have done but to listen to the questions and suggestions of key employees. These discussions can only improve the formulation of the future strategy. This meeting will also serve as a way to begin the process of generating employee commitment to a new strategy.

Chapter Summary

- You created a Core Strategy Team to guide the organization through a careful and honest examination of organizational assumptions and the program gaps that exist as a consequence of those presumptions.
- After taking inventory of all programs, you compared actual results against mission and vision driven desired outcomes.
- You identified:
  o Program gaps
  o Resource gaps
  o Different types of clients of your services
  o Core competencies
  o The competition
  o How organizations with similar missions deliver services
- You learned how to conduct:
  o Google analysis
  o Process audit
  o Capabilities audit
- You gathered comprehensive information about your nonprofit's strengths and weaknesses.

CHAPTER FIVE

Designing the Future

In this chapter you will create your future:

- Frame your future identity
- Create choice-making opportunities
- Evaluate organizational implications
- Develop maps to guide the nonprofit

Framing the Nonprofit's Future Identity

As you go forward in this process, keep two things in mind. (1) The purpose of strategic planning is to uncover buried problems (problems that have been continually ignored, or in some case, not visible to the organization) while creating an alternative hypotheses about the future role of the organization. (2) The future will not look like today or yesterday. It is important, therefore, to question your organization's conventional assumptions about its services, products, and client community. The data you have collected will prove or disprove these accepted norms.

The next step is to schedule and hold an ALL-DAY MEETING WORKSHOP with your Core Strategy Team. During the morning portion of this workshop, you will synthesize and debate data and then formulate insights (keep minutes of discussions). Keep in mind that the discussions and insights generated during the workshop are as important to the process as the hard data you have already collected. Your insights will help you transform your current situation into a desired future.

Workshop Morning Session – Summarize Analytics

- ➢ From **Table 19 Summary Chart 1**: What insights have you gained about the costs and revenues associated with your programs as well as their impact on mission? How sustainable is it for your organization to keep delivering these programs in the same fashion?
- ➢ From **Table 20 Summary Chart 2**: What insights have you gained about your organization's capacity to meet its mission? How does organizational capacity match up against your mission?
- ➢ From **Tables 21 – 33 Summary Charts 3**: What insights have you gained about how your stakeholders perceive your organization? Do they see it the same way as you do? What are the commonalities?
- ➢ From **Table 34 Summary Chart 4**: What have you learned about the hole in the universe that would open should your organization go out of business today? Would there be a hole?
- ➢ From **Table 35 Summary Chart 5**: What have you learned about how the outside world thinks of your organization – or if they even know you exist.
- ➢ From **Table 37**: What insights have you gained as to programs and services that are in direct competition with your organization. The competitors in the HH quadrant on the landscape map are the programs you should discuss the most.
- ➢ From **Tables 39, 41, 43**: What insights have you gained as to how other organizations (not competing in your field) deliver value to their client community? Would any of their delivery methods be appropriate for your organization?

By now you should have a good feel for:

- what your organization does well
- what your organization does not do so well
- what holes exist in your programming
- what the world thinks of your organization
- what competition you face
- your organization's financial situation

Workshop Afternoon Session - Option Development

DISCUSSION: Imagine that it is five years from now. The lead story in the New York Times is about the top three nonprofits in the world. Your organization is one of the three. For this future to come true; what programs will you need to deliver? How will they need to be delivered? What did you accomplish to be recognized as a top organization? Reverse engineer your products or services. When and what processes and resources did you use to create their success.

KEY PRIORITIES: In order to operationalize your choices, you will need to establish a few key priorities. These are the must-haves that serve as the foundation for organizational mission and goal setting. Engage the team in discussion with the following questions:

1. What problem(s) will the organization be most interested in solving in the next five years?
2. Who will the organization serve – the primary client community? What will the client avatar look like in five years?
3. What core competencies must the organization excel at five years from now?
4. What is the best way to use these core competencies to solve our future client community's problem?
5. What changes are required from your organization to move forward?

Use Table 44 as template to summarize your findings.

Table 44 Summarize Priority Findings

Problem(s) to be solved?	
Primary client community?	
Core competencies organization will excel at into the future?	
How will core competencies solve client community's problem?	
Changes required from organization to move forward?	

Creating Choices

With key priorities established, think about three promising opportunities for further exploration? Think big! For this exercise, forget about negative deconstructive talk, forget about limited resources. You will have opportunities to do that later in this process. Instead, focus on ideal solutions. As an organization, you already know what you can do, and what you have done in the past. It is time now to focus on what you want to do in the future to solve your mission problem. Use following charts to investigate further.

Table 45 Create Choices, #1

Opportunity 1:
Potential Mission Impact:
Value to Client Community:
Capabilities Needed:

Table 46 Create Choices, #2

Opportunity 2:
Potential Mission Impact:
Value to Client Community:
Capabilities Needed:

Table 47 Create Choices, #3

Opportunity 3:
Potential Mission Impact:
Value to Client Community:
Capabilities Needed:

Organizational Implications - Assessment of Opportunities

This would be a good time to convene key staff who are not members of the Core Strategy Team to review findings to date. Share key priorities and potential opportunities for the organization's future. It is not only important to share what you have done but to listen to the questions and suggestions of key employees. These discussions can only improve the formulation of the future strategy. This meeting will also serve as a way to continue the process of generating employee commitment to a new strategy. When the Core Strategy Team reconvenes, reassess the three opportunities using feedback from key staff meeting. Keep in mind that change, even the talk about it, tends to make people feel uneasy. If your staff is feeling uneasy this is a sign that you are making progress toward a better future. If your people are feeling too comfortable about future opportunities, chances are you have not deviated from the status quo.

Let us now begin to look deeper at the potential future opportunities. Using **Tables 48, 49, and 50**, ask your Core Strategy Team to visualize, discuss, and record the ideal conditions necessary to make each opportunity a reality. Focus only on what needs to take place and not on your organization's current ability to make the opportunity real. Remember, you want to think big; think different in order to create your desired future.

Table 48 Ideal Conditions, #1

Opportunity 1:
For this to be successful, the following questions will need to be answered (still not the time to argue feasibility of opportunity):
Partners needed?
Systems needed to deliver services?

Resources needed:
    • Human
    • Time
    • Facilities
    • Technology
    • Other (non-financial)

How big should we be?
How will we measure success?

Table 49 Ideal Conditions, #2

Opportunity 2:
For this to be successful, the following questions will need to be answered (still not the time to argue feasibility of opportunity):
Partners needed?
Systems needed to deliver services?
Resources needed: <ul><li>Human</li><li>Time</li><li>Facilities</li><li>Technology</li><li>Other (non-financial)</li></ul>
How big should we be?
How will we measure success?

Table 50 Ideal Conditions, #3

Opportunity 3:
For this to be successful, the following questions will need to be answered (still not the time to argue feasibility of opportunity):
Partners needed?
Systems needed to deliver services?
Resources needed: • Human • Time • Facilities • Technology • Other (non-financial)
How big should we be?
How will we measure success?

We will use the following framework as a focal point for strategy development.

Figure 10 Framework for New Strategy

Impact Potential

> The strategy must create measurable impact
> Strategy addresses both mission and vision for future
> Difficulty in implementing strategy must be achievable
> If needed, strategy is scalable to fit different client communities
> Strategy contributes to creating a positive public image

Financial

> Strategy must be economically sustainable
> Revenue streams must be plausible, not made-up

High-Quality Programs

> Does your organization currently have the skills to excel in this strategy
> How difficult would it be to acquire the essential skills needed to carry the strategy
> Strategy builds on organizations' core competencies and strengths
> What partners (existing or new) could be involved in strategy

Make Choices

Now that you have created your dream future, it is the time to determine how well your organization can support the vision. The first step in the process will be to conduct an overview feasibility study on EACH of the three future opportunities. There is no sense creating goals before you know if your aspiration has the potential for reality or if it is just a pipe dream. Refer to the **New Strategy Framework (Figure 10)** to guide your discussions.

Figure 11 Feasibility Template

Technical Feasibility:
1. What format will deliver new opportunity?
2. Number of clients who benefit?
3. Who are your competitors in this space?
4. What facilities and/or materials will be needed?
5. Is it needed?
6. Is it sustainable?
7. Has anyone else tried this concept? How did it turnout?
8. What technology will be required?

Financial Feasibility:
1. Forecast expense of new opportunity
2. Forecast revenue of new opportunity
3. Forecast cash flow needs of new opportunity
4. Forecast overall financial viability of new opportunity

Organizational Feasibility:
1. Who will be the key people needed to implement new opportunity?
2. What processes do you have that lend to new opportunity?
3. What processes will you need to create?
4. Overall, how difficult will it be to acquire the core competencies needed to implement new opportunity?

After you have completed the feasibility studies, convene key staff who are not members of the Core Strategy Team to share your analysis on the three potential opportunities (if three are still viable). It is not only important to disclose what you have done but to listen to the questions and suggestions of key employees. This meeting will also serve as a way to continue the process of generating employee commitment to a new strategy.

Table 51Key Staff Feedback, Opportunity 1

Opportunity #1

Technical Feasibility:

Financial Feasibility:

Organizational Feasibility:

Table 52 Key Staff Feedback, Opportunity 2

<u>Opportunity #2</u>

Technical Feasibility:

Financial Feasibility:

Organizational Feasibility:

Table 53 Key Staff Feedback, Opportunity 3

<u>Opportunity #3</u>

Technical Feasibility:

Financial Feasibility:

Organizational Feasibility:

When the Core Strategy Team reconvenes, reassess the three opportunities using feedback from key staff meeting.

Based on all of your discussions and analysis, <u>choose</u> the most promising opportunity to move your organization into the future. Use **Table 54** to guide your thinking

Table 54 the Big Opportunity

Name of new opportunity:
The new opportunity is (describe):
It will serve this many clients?
How will it help clients?
How will it help us?
How is it different from what we currently do?
What are unique benefits of this opportunity?
What major risks are associated with opportunity?
What financial bucket (G, BE, I. S) does this opportunity fall?
The total estimated cost of the opportunity: • Year one? • Year three? • Year five?
The total estimated revenue: • Year one? • Year three? • Year five?

Business Continuity and Disaster Recovery Planning

Organizational Exercise 7	CHALLENGE: If the nonprofit headquarters building went up in a blazing inferno overnight, could the nonprofit survive? Discuss with Core Strategy Team.

Effective organizations must be prepared for disasters. They are inevitable and can occur at any time. Disasters can take many forms. It could be a storm such as a hurricane or tornado, an earthquake, landside or fire. More likely, the organization will be a victim of a cyber-attack. Even minor misfortunes such as an extended power failure or a broken water main can have an adverse effect on the nonprofit. All of these things disrupt operations. How much they do depends on your planning – or lack of it.

Before we start the planning process, let's define business continuity and disaster recovery – the two plans you need. Although they appear to be the same thing and both can shut the organization down, for planning purposes we use the following definitions.

- Business Continuity Planning is directed at people, processes, and property.
- Disaster Recovery Planning is all about technology, data, and business applications.

Step one for both business continuity and disaster recovery planning, answer (as organization) the following questions – commonly known as business impact analysis.

1. What disasters could occur? Rate them for likelihood.
2. What programs and services have the highest risks?

3. What services or programs are of strategic importance to the nonprofit? Rate them on priority.
4. Which business processes are indispensable to the strategic services and programs?
5. For each disaster, what impact would they have on the nonprofit financially? On clients?
6. What is the maximum allowable timeline acceptable to reach full recovery?

Step two: develop the business continuity plan.

1. Create crisis management team (assign project leader) to develop plans
2. Crisis team to develop incident response plan outlining people and processes needed to address initial response to disaster. The goal of these first responders is to stop or soften the impact of the incident using a set of predetermined procedures and strategies. Their role is to also collect and provide data the organization needs to fully recover. Forecast financial costs, resources, and communication needs of the first responders. Also include offsite meeting places for team and responders to meet in the event that office locations are not accessible.
3. Review and update insurance policies. Know what is covered and under what circumstances.
4. Crisis team to develop incident recovery plan outlining resources and people needed to achieve full recovery. Include timelines, budget, communications, and alternative modes of service and program delivery. The idea is to develop a pre-defined set of responses that enable the nonprofit to react quickly and effectively.
5. When holding or sponsoring a convention, always purchase Act of God insurance. Nature doesn't abide by your timelines.
6. Train staff and test plans – look for holes or gaps that need to be addressed.

7. Review plans quarterly
8. Develop an organizational policy, if you don't have one, authorizing spokespersons who are permitted to speak to the news media. You want one informed voice speaking to the media and your client community. Your policy will determine in advance who talks to the media during a crisis. For each potential disaster you have identified, create a set of talking points allowing your spokesperson to deliver clear and practical information without having to improvise under pressure. Talking points will buy the organization time to collect and analyze data before announcing the recovery plan.
9. Develop individualized communication talking points for the following audiences:
   a. Clients
   b. Employee
   c. Vendors and suppliers
   d. Neighbors in your community
   e. Press
   f. Social media
   g. Board of Directors – current and past

Step three: develop the disaster recovery plan.

1. Because disaster recovery involves technical equipment such as servers and networks, it is important to create a DR Crisis Team that has the technical knowledge and knowhow to address these issues. If the nonprofit does not employ individuals with these skills, ask your vendors or local experts to volunteer to assist with the creation of the plan. You want a plan that describes how the nonprofit should respond to identified incidents.
2. Using the Business Impact Analysis as the starting point for identifying technology-related risks.
3. DR Crisis Team should review past unplanned disruptions and how they were resolved.

4. DR Crisis Team will need to inventory age and life expectancy of all technical equipment.

5. DR Crisis Team will need to create a first responder team outlining people and processes needed to address initial response to the disaster. The goal of these first responders is to stop or soften the impact of the incident using a set of predetermined procedures and strategies. Also, include offsite meeting places for team and responders to meet in the event that office locations are not accessible.

6. DR Crisis Team to develop recovery plan outlining resources and people needed to achieve full recovery. Include timelines, budget, communications, and alternative modes of service and program delivery.

7. DR Crisis Team to propose contingency budget which can be used if disaster strikes.

8. Follow steps 8 and 9 from Business Continuity Plan

Figure 12 Sample Business Impact Analysis

Classify impact of each event on nonprofit as:
- Negligible – no significant loss
- Major – impacts one or more services or programs
- Crisis – has significant financial or material impact

Disaster Event	Likelihood (L,M,H)	Services At Risk	Steps to Prevent	Impact on Nonprofit
Cyber-attack				
Server failure				
Fire				
Power failure				
Hurricane				
Tornado				
Winter storm				
Supplier failure				
Cash flow shortage				
Other				

Chapter Summary

- Your team reviewed the data and findings from Chapter 4 and created options for the future.
- After exploring several promising opportunities, your team conducted feasibility studies on each.
- You developed business continuity and disaster recovery plans.
- The team selected your next big opportunity and the organization is now ready to develop goals, objectives, and budgets.

CHAPTER SIX

Invent the Future

Goals, Objectives, & Unit Strategies

Now for a moment, think of the process a young couple goes through when planning their wedding. In many cases, the bride may have an aspiration for the dream wedding day. That vision may include a traditional church wedding, a destination wedding, a city hall wedding, or any variation imaginable. After they become engaged, the future bride and groom will discuss, debate, and share their vision of a dream wedding. They will eventually examine their particular life circumstances, and consider whether or not they can make the vision of a dream wedding come true. Let us assume they have decided the vision is achievable. This is where you are with your organization's strategy. You believe it to be achievable and are ready to move forward with making it a reality.

You will now need to define specific organizational goals to carry your plan forward. Keep in mind these goals need to be a connector from past practices to future processes. In other words, you are building a bridge from the present to the future. Your employees, the ones who will ultimately carry out the strategy, need to see how their daily work is changing and how their work is transforming the organization's future. (Your organization cannot just stop what it is currently doing while waiting for the future. You are still responsible for delivering on the mission today as well as on tomorrow's mission. But know you must keep the implementing of new goals in the forefront of organizational activity.) In the case of the wedding couple, let's say they chose a destination wedding. One of their goals might be to give their wedding guests nine months advance notice of the wedding to allow guests to make financial and vacation arrangements. The couple recognizes that guests need to make ends meet today while planning for the future wedding.

Fill in the Blanks

You now have an organizational premonition, you can see what the future looks like. The only thing left is for you to fill in the details that will transport you from the present to the desired future. Begin by listing the three to five broad goals you will need to achieve in order to make your new vision a reality. The goals may be along the lines of the following: to be the leading expert organization in your field; to provide superior products and services that make a significant difference in the lives of our client community; to create a sustainable budget that allows for program exploration and growth; or to increase organization's reach to an under-represented client community.

Once you have determined your goals you will want to develop organizational objectives. This is where you will need to be specific and detailed. Your Core Strategy Team will want to develop three or four organizational objectives for each goal. For example, let us imagine that your organization is a membership association that produces journals and newsletters. One organizational goal might be to build a robust, database-driven content management system to increase member engagement. Corresponding objectives might be as follows:

(1)   Convert print journals A,B,C to online & tablet ready format

(2)   Re-launch association newsletter into a fully functional online publication

(3)   Establish an online content acquisition platform connecting authors and editors in real time

Now is the time to connect actions to your choices. To do this, you will need the help of all employees —not just the core team. You must now challenge each unit, or division, in your organization to develop a set of strategies that align that units' actions with the organizational goals and objectives. This is one of the most important steps in the process. Without the input and support of your front line employees your efforts to develop a new plan with be for naught as your strategic plan will become nothing more than an archival document gathering dust in your organization's library.

As each unit or division discusses and develops specific strategies to connect their work with the organization's goals, it would be a good idea for each unit to create a one-page Unit Strategic Map that connects unit strategies with activities and accountability.

When developing unit strategies, unit leaders will want to focus on incorporating new activities into already used departmental operating procedures. To map out a strategic unit plan, address the following questions:

- What key processes, technology, people, information, resources are required by the unit to deliver against unit strategy and organizational goals?
- What metrics will the unit use to measure success against the unit strategy and organizational goals?
- What things will we need to stop doing?

Figure 13 Elements of One Page Unit Strategic Map

ORGANIZATIONAL GOALS

• List of organizational goals that connect directly to department

ORGANIZATIONAL OBJECTIVES

• List of measurable targets attached to achieving each goal

UNIT STRATEGIES

• List how departmental and organizational resources will be used to achieve goal

UNIT ACCOUNTABILITY

• Clear identification of the work that will be

Figure 14 Example One Page Unit Strategic Map

Goal: Build a robust, database-driven content management system to increase member engagement
Objectives: A. Convert print journals A,B,C to online & tablet ready format B. Establish an online content acquisition platform connecting authors and editors in real time

Activity	Responsible Units	Start Date	End Date	Estimate Cost	Strategies
Convert print journals to online & tablet ready	Publications Anne, John Sarah, Jim IT Tim, Harry Dillon, Mary Tina Marketing George Martha	Jul 1 2016	Jun 30 2017	$750,000	• Create digital platform from scratch • Train editors on digital submission platform • Prepare market campaign for client community • Convert archives from print to digital • Create digital journal components
Re-launch association newsletter into a functional online publication	Publications Anne, Anita Ralph IT Martha Murry	Jul 1 2016	Mar 31 2017	$150,000	• Upgrade web content system • Integrate with AMS system • Redesign membership section of web
Establish an online content acquisition platform connecting authors and editors in real time	Publication Sarah, Sam Research Terrie IT Jim	Jul 1 2016	Dec 31 2016	$75,000	• Identify existing CMS in field • Seek IT advice: development of software solution vs purchase software • Determine training needs for authors & editors

In order to move an organization in a new direction, two more important steps are needed. The first is rather simple. Each unit must share their strategy map with every other unit within the organization. This is important for these reasons.

(1)   The unit map serves as an informal communication tool. It conveys to all employee's how each unit will participate in creating the desired future.

(2)   The unit map can also serve as a tool to enlist cross-unit participation in creating client community solutions and innovations.

(3)   The unit map should reduce, or eliminate organizational redundancies.

(4)   Sharing promotes a healthy culture, encouraging teamwork and collaboration

The second step necessary is to align each individual employee's work with the unit strategies and greater organizational goals. The strategy must be clear for every job, ensuring all employees' understand how their work connects to organizational priorities.   To align individual employee job tasks with organizational goals, unit leaders must work with their staff to create individual strategy maps.

Individual Strategy Maps

Chances are good that many employees do not know how their work is connected to overall organizational success. Unfortunately, many employees go through each day mindlessly performing tasks without knowing how those tasks impact the organizational mission. Unit leaders, supervisors, managers, and executives can correct this after strategic unit maps have been created by working with each employee to create their own strategic map. This is not an employee performance review, but rather a personal road map to show

how to connect day-to-day work with the unit strategy and organizational goals.

The Individual Strategy Map will connect employee insights, experiences, and talents with the day-to-day work that comprises the organizational strategic plan. To achieve this:

- Each employee should have a list of personal and measurable objectives to be met over the next 12 months
- Each employee should have a list (and the resources) of everything they need from the organization to meet those goals
- Each employee's supervisor should be committed to providing the employee with the resources needed to meet those goals.
- Train employees to constantly ask:

  - ✓ How does this activity – routine day-to-day work - benefit the client community? Create revenue? Add expense? Meet organizational strategic goal?
  - ✓ Why am I doing this task this way? Is there a better way to get this done? Does it contribute to the unit strategy?
  - ✓ Does anyone else in the organization do this task? Could it be done better in another unit more effectively? Is it necessary? Why?

Figure 15 Example Individual Employee Strategy Map

Organizational Goal: Build a robust, database-driven content management system to increase member engagement
Unit: Membership
Employee: Vince
Supervisor: Jill

Goal	Activity	Resources Needed	G	Y	S
1. Select AMS	1. Participate on AMS Selection Team	Time			
	2. Identify department specifications	Departmental co-workers			
2. Website Integration	1. Create departmental microsites	IT support & co-workers			
	2. Create member portal	It support, co-workers			
3. Member Blogs	1. Create and configure functional member blog	Time, Editors, IT support			
	2. Select volunteers to monitor blog	Network of volunteers			
	3. Merge existing listserv into blog	IT support			
	4. Build servers to host blog	IT support			
4. Member Database	1. Tie all member Purchases to database	IT support, co-workers			
	2.Dedupe duplicate member accounts	IT support			
	3. Integrate association store accounts with membership database	IT support			
5. Demographic Tracking	1. Prepare to integrate all new membership campaigns with AMS	Time, outside vendor, IT support			
	2. Develop and insert tracking codes in all mailings & ads	Co-workers, marketing, publications			
6. List other Goals	List activities for each additional goal				

Legend

G = Go, Progress on Target

Y = Yield, Caution, in danger of failing

R = Red, Progress failing

Your strategic plan is your roadmap into the future and tells the world of your intentions. For your employees to carry out these intentions they need a visible reminder to help them make those tough decisions about what to do, and what to stop doing.

- Every employee should have a copy of the organization's strategic plan visible at their workstation.
- The strategic plan should be summarized in chart form of no more than 1 page. Laminating the chart for use as a desk pad or to be hung as a calendar would be useful.
- In addition to the organizational strategic plan, it is important that supervisors, managers, and executives talk about the plan during regularly scheduled staff meetings. The more often employees hear about what is and what is not part of the plan, the better they will understand and implement the plan.

Example of One Page Strategic Plan can be found on the next page.

Figure 16 Example One Page Strategic Plan

Mission	Organizational Objectives
Rehabilitate houses in South Central Chicago for low income tenants	*Community Outreach* 1. To achieve 30% of tenants who participate in monthly town meetings by 2020 2. To implement a Community Home Owners program through the training of community tenant leaders within two years
Vision South Central Chicago: a safe, drug-free, family community	*Funding* 1. Partner with the Walmart Foundation, the Home Depot Foundation to provide building and housing materials at low or no cost 2. Enlist regional & national celebrities to advocate on behalf of ABCXYZ
Core Values *Integrity* – consistently acts in the best interest of the client community, co-workers, and the organization. *Excellence* – holds self and co-workers accountable for results. *Compassion* – treats co-workers, client community, & vendors with respect	*Membership* 1. Increase first-year retention rate from 50% to 65% by year 3 of plan 2. Increase member average attendance at monthly meetings by 20% in year 3 3. Increase volunteer opportunities to participate in both pre and post rehab
Organizational Goals 1. *Community Outreach*: provide new services to support the local community 2. *Funding*: create sustainable funding model 3. *Membership*: increase growth, retention, and engagement 4. *Networking*: collaborate with strategic partners 5. *Education*: provide client community & volunteers opportunities to learn about home ownership	*Networking* 1. Work with local schools to provide a safe, educationally stimulating before & after school programs for children of South Central Chicago 2. Partner with public and private organizations on behalf of issues facing South Central Chicago *Education* 1. To implement a project to develop employment skills in unemployed adults 2. To implement a program that provides do-it-yourself training for common home maintenance 3. To provide members of the community such assistance that is within the capabilities. of ABCXYZ to prepare them to take full responsibility for home ownership

Chapter Summary

In this chapter you learned how to develop:

- One page Unit/Department Strategy Map
- One page Individual Employee Strategy Map
- One page Strategic Plan

Some final words about strategic thinking and planning. You will want to:

- Create an **ongoing vigilant management practice** of monitoring, examining, and developing the programs needed to close gaps between the work you think you are doing and the work the organization is actually performing (many of the procedures used throughout strategic planning. can be incorporated into regular, routine operations)
- Avoid **mission creep** – those subtle activities not related to organizational strategy that find their way into the operations process
- Regularly **engage your employees'** – all of them – in dialogue about mission hits and misses
- Strategic thinking is an **ongoing process** that should never stop

CHAPTER SEVEN

Building a Budget for the Future

Introduction

The mission is the reason the nonprofit exists. It should clearly state the social problem your organization is trying to solve. During the day-to-day operations, it is easy to lose sight of the stated mission strategy and to expand services outside of the intended strategic parameters. It happens all the time, even to the best of organizations. It is in the nature of people to want to solve problems; to want to do good deeds for others. This is why it is important to visit with the mission and vision statements on a regular basis. Eliminating stray paths before they become institutionalized and consume the valuable and limited resources of the nonprofit is essential if the nonprofit is to remain true to its core mission. Mission creep and blurred vision can really take a toll on your annual budget as you find yourself funding programs and services that, although may be worthy, don't match your stated mission and strategy. Be vigilant about sticking with your core mission strategy as change can happen unexpectedly and unnoticed.

Be watchful of changes that can occur within your client community. Change can mean your clients no longer need the same support as they received before. They may need more, less or something different. For example, The Global Polio Eradication Initiative was created in 1988 to eradicate the world of polio. Their initial strategy was to immunize all of the world's children. By 2013 2.5 billion children had been vaccinated against polio and all but a few countries were polio free. At some point in time, the Global Polio Eradication Initiative may just achieve its mission on eradicating polio. When that happens, their mission may change from eradication to education and prevention. Your organization's mission may need changing as well. Perhaps there are other agencies in your field who can provide better services, or perhaps the needs of your client community is shifting to another area. The point of this discussion is to make you aware of a world in constant change. Pay close attention the world your clients live in.

Elements of a Good Annual Budget Plan

1. Your annual budget should focus on the priorities addressed in the strategic plan. This is important for several reasons:

   a. Without a budget built around a vision priority, staff confusion as to what is important and what is not becomes an issue and ultimately allows employees to choose a priority. There can be no individual choices when it comes to organization priority. All department and employees must work on the same priority if the organization is to achieve success.

   b. Lack of vision priority means using resources on activities that are not a priority, making organizational success more difficult, or even impossible to achieve

2. Identify strategic and high priority program goals. Be sure to attach measurable results to each program goal. This step is important for several reasons:

   a. Limited resources –the organization cannot pursue every idea, no matter how noble. The focus must be

on the strategic priority goals that propel your
organization into the future

b. Measurable results are necessary to monitor progress
   toward achieving vision

3. Organizational Revenue - you must be able to forecast
   annual revenue. What number will the actual,
   predictable revenue generate?

   a. The emphasis must be on reachable revenue, which
      will most likely be different from desired revenue

4. Organizational Expenses - you must be able to analyze
   annual expenses. This element may be the most difficult,
   and most important, for the future of your organization.
   Before you allocate resources, you will need to make
   some decisions about operations and future
   programming.

5. Which top priorities will you fund?

   a. Which programs currently funded may need to be
      scaled down, up, or eliminated? Remember
      Einstein's Theory of Insanity. Change is necessary for
      successful organizational growth.

Getting Started

Budget planning for nonprofits can be very confusing.
Unknowingly, departments often compete against each other
and the organization's vision and mission for scarce resources.
Staffs struggle with understanding where the money comes
from and where it goes. And in many instances, employees fail
to connect budgeting with the organization's strategy, mission,
and vision. Help staff to connect the dots.

And just as surprising, many nonprofit organizations fail to
create program metrics to measure success against

revenue/expense ratios. Many nonprofits build their budgets on blind faith and unqualified aspirations. They hope to earn a little more than the year before while maintaining the same institutional footprint. This strategy – or lack of strategy – rarely turns out well. Costs tend to rise each year regardless of any conscious cost cutting measures. Health insurance goes up, supplies cost more, and service vendors adjust prices as well. And nonprofits end their fiscal year disappointed. Establish clear metrics for each program.

The nonprofit budget is the highway for the organization's mission and vision. It delivers money, staff, and time to achieve the organization's strategy. Budgeting allows the organization to think about the future – to consider new opportunities and new difficulties. On a more practical level, the budget prescribes the day-to-day actions needed to move the organization in a forward direction by coordinating activities and staff responsibilities. The budget also serves as a management control tool. In order for your nonprofit to keep its doors open it must produce enough revenue to cover expenses. When done correctly, the budget will contain benchmarks for measuring mission accomplishments against revenue and expenses. The benchmarks serve as stop, cautionary, or go signs for those who are accountable and responsible for delivery of a program or service.

Budgeting should be done thoughtfully, meaningfully, and with an eye on strategy and mission growth. It is not hard constructing a useful annual budget but it does require more than financial planning. It requires patience and most importantly, all employees to think like one organization. Budget building requires all employee work to be connected to a budget line item. No organizational work should be performed without a direct and corresponding detailed link to the annual budget. What follows is an outlined approach of developing a budget that embeds both cost management and revenue into employee day-to-day workflow. Along with a mission driven strategic budget, you will create a culture which demystifies budgets while enabling all staff to fully participate in organizational decision-making.

Types of Budget

There are two acceptable types of budgets – both should be aligned with vision and strategy:

1. Traditional – based on analysis of past performance and then projecting future performance based on current environmental and operational conditions. Traditional budgets start by assessing the financial performance of all programs and services over the previous two or three years noting trends or patterns.   This allows managers to see the financial effectiveness of each program as well as to develop financial forecasting models. (Target for overall organization operating efficiency should be 75% to 110%. Operating efficiency is total revenue divided by total assets.)

2. Zero-based – designing a new budget without historical performance. All future services and programs document and verify every expected source of revenue and expenses for the coming budget cycle.

Unfortunately, there is another type of budgeting used by many nonprofits - a percentage budget. With this type of budgeting, the nonprofit simply assigns a small percentage (+/- 3%) increase in all revenues and expenses. This process involves no thinking, no planning, and no evaluation of current and past performance. This is flying by the seat of your pants. Instinct will only take you so far before failure takes hold and brings the nonprofit down.

Budget Categories

Nonprofit budgets are generally partitioned into two categories:

1. Discretionary – defines potential new projects, programs, improvements, upgrades – any program or service where management has choices to make.
2. Non-discretionary – designates fixed expenses such as utilities, rent, equipment, insurance, essential programs, staff, payroll taxes, health benefits, etc. Non-discretionary items are things where no choice is involved – you simply must pay to stay in existence.

Keep in mind, you influence the non-discretionary budget with the choices you make in the discretionary budget. For example, if you eliminate or scale back a program you might need fewer paid staff. Reducing staff lowers payroll and benefits. Increasing staff raises compensation. It is important to recognize that the discretionary and non-discretionary portions of the budget complement each other. When you add or subtract from one, you will need to add or subtract from the other in order to create a balanced budget.

Each new fiscal year requires a budget that directs revenue and spending activities for each program and service. Generally, nonprofits spend the last three to four months of the current fiscal year creating budget projections for each activity (Including revenue, costs, and margin projections) and determining where resources and time are required. In many instances, this is a top-down process whereby upper management, or the CFO, develop the numbers for next year's budget. If you are creating a budget using this method – STOP. Here is why:

1. All employees make routine spending decisions every day (even if they are not aware of it). Front-line

employees, as well as supervisors, need to fully understand where the money comes from and where it goes.

2. Openly sharing accurate information and basing decisions on a common set of numbers encourages interactions between units, leading to efficient processes and better programs and services.

3. In order to hold employees accountable for budgeted results, they must fully understand (not necessarily agree with) all budget modifications to their respective budgets. While consensus in the budget process may be impossible to achieve, inclusion in the decision-making process and full disclosure regarding budget assumptions and modifications will empower employees to manage their daily work in a more fiscally responsible manner and will place accountability for budgeted results squarely upon the shoulders of supervisors, managers, and executive leadership.

Budgeting is a year-long and continuous process and is grounded on creating deep knowledge of organizational expense drivers and revenue producers, and using that knowledge to manage product/service performance. The day-to-day decisions made by all employees produce actionable budget data – information that should be shared and discussed in terms of money well spent, or money not meeting strategic goals. These discussions should be included in your monthly strategy meetings. What you learn about cost management throughout the year becomes the foundation upon which the next budget is built.

You should think of the budget as an integrated part of strategy and operations rather than as a standalone means to an ends. The objective is to "talk" about money as you generate new ideas for improving programs and services. In this case "talk" means active investigation and research. Too often, ideas are brought up during the year and summarily dismissed – without any homework performed - because someone believes the idea will cost too much. Maybe it will, maybe it won't; you will never know unless your plug some numbers into the Excel Workbook. The point is, you need to start somewhere if you expect to develop raw ideas into operations. Engage in these discussions all year long.

Preliminary Budget Work: Financial Reporting System

1. Chart of Accounts (COA)

The chart of accounts is the core structure for classifying and recording financial transactions, organizing your financial information and how it is reported to the community. Each entry records transactions with a set of codes that represent expenses or revenues by function. The design of the COA must be planned well to fit current management needs while addressing potential future requirements. Your budget structure must match the CAO; if not, you will track and record the wrong financial information leading to costly decisions. The COA should also be matched with your Statement of Financial Position and the IRS 990.

The COA:

- Is a chronological log of transactions measured in monetary terms to match budget documents with COA
- Supports your organization's fiscal policy and is a key tool in managing the budget
- Allows you to monitor liabilities and all liquid assets
- Is the basis for internal controls and day-to-day decision making

- Should meet the information and reporting requirements needed to support bot budget and accounting frameworks while avoiding redundancy

You will have the following five accounts set up in your COA:

1. Asset   = something you own
2. Liability = something you owe
3. Equity   = your overall worth
4. Income   = money you get
5. Expense = money you spend

The Unified Chart of Accounts for nonprofit organizations looks like:	
Assets	1000-1999
Liabilities	2000-2999
Equity	3000-3999
Contributions	4000-4999
Earned Revenue	5000-5999
Other Revenue	6000-6999
Employee Related Expenses	7000-7999
Non-Employee Related Expenses	8000-8999
Non GAAP Expenses	9000-9999

2. Cash vs Accrual

These are the two methods of keeping track of expenses and revenues. The difference between the two is the timing of when transactions are credited or debited to your account. Here's how each works:

Cash basis - income is not counted until cash (including checks, money orders, etc.) is actually received, and expenses are not counted until they are actually paid.

Accrual basis - transactions are counted when the order or service is provided, regardless of when the money for them is actually received. Income is counted when the service occurs; expenses are counted when you receive the goods or services rather than when you pay for it.

Advantages of cash basis method: it provides a more accurate picture of how much actual cash your nonprofit has.

Disadvantages of cash basis method: it may offer a misleading picture of longer-term profitability. For example, your books may show one month to be highly profitable, when actually services have been slow and, by coincidence, a lot of clients paid their bills in that month.

Advantages of accrual method: it shows the up and down flow of income and expenses more accurately

Disadvantages of the accrual method: it may leave not show you what cash reserves are available, which could result in a serious cash flow problem

Accrual basis accounting lends itself to better budgeting because it looks at when expenses are incurred and revenue is earned.

Which Method to Use?

The cash basis is the easiest, but not necessarily the most accurate. It is best used with a small nonprofit with few, if any, paid staff and no intentions of growing.

The accrual basis should be used by any nonprofit with paid staff, large amounts of revenue, and plans to continue raising funds from donors. Accrual is required for auditing under GAAP (Generally Accepted Accounting Principles).

Regardless of which method you choose (most nonprofits will use accrual), it is a good idea to look at the data through both lenses in order to get a complete picture of your nonprofit's health. Additionally, I recommend you use a rolling budget

Under a rolling budget, performance of the operation over the last 12 months is evaluated on an on-going basis; projections for the next three months are generated every month.

3. Rolling Budget

Most nonprofits use a traditional twelve-month budget. If you use this method consider moving to a rolling budget. Under a rolling budget, the next three months are generated at the end of each quarter keeping your master budget as a static twelve-month tool. Your budget will always cover the next twelve months. The advantage of this method is staff and management will continue to assess and evaluate programs results against budget estimates. Your team will be more agile and adept at making program corrections in the present rather than waiting six, nine, or twelve months down the road to act. Time and money are your allies and should be spent wisely.

The disadvantage of the rolling budget is the training and mindset changes needed to implement the method. You want to be careful that staff does not view a rolling budget as a constant focus on numbers at the expense of providing services and programs. Done well, a rolling budget supports decision-making and is integrated into the daily routines of staff. When done well, a rolling budget is not more time consuming than a traditional budget, rather, it is more time spent learning and managing the revenue and expense drivers of the organization.

4. Establish Priorities

Set one to three organizational priorities as prescribed by mission, vision, and strategic plans. Mission creep has a way of draining resources while distorting organization vision. Organizational priorities create the framework needed to promote culture and product improvement; strategic thinking; and the alignment of all work with the organization's vision.

Before establishing priorities, visit with your mission, vision, and core value statements ensuring they reflect the desired future direction of the nonprofit. If they don't, spend time with staff updating the statements as they serve as the foundation of the budget. Be sure your statements are aligned with your organization's strategic plan

5. Assess Program and Service Performance

Assess financial performance of all programs and services over the previous five years. Take note of trends or patterns. This step will help you see the financial effectiveness of each program as well as to develop financial forecasting models. You will find the following Statements helpful with your review:

- Financial Activities
- Financial Activities, Month-to-Month
- Departmental Expenses
- Modified Functional Expenses

6. Assess Financial Performance

Assess financial performance of all programs and services over the previous five years (Figures 25, 29). Take note of trends or patterns. This step will help you see the financial effectiveness of each program as well as to develop financial forecasting models. (Target for overall organization operating efficiency of all programs should be 75% to 110%. Operating efficiency is total revenue divided by total assets.) You will need the following Statements from Chapter I of this book:

- Financial Activities (Figures 8, 9)
- Financial Activities, Month-to-Month (Figure 10)
- Departmental Expenses (Figure13)
- Modified Functional Expenses (Figure 14)

Assign each program into one of four buckets. The four buckets are:

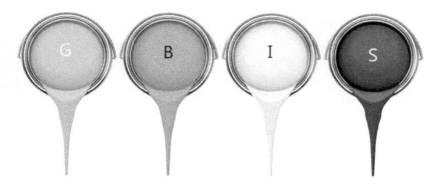

Generate revenue – programs that produce positive income. Total must create enough profit for the organization to pay for the Invest and subsidize activities at year end

Break-even – cover all costs (including overhead) associated with running the programs. Many times these programs provide services to other departments through charge-backs.

Invest – new initiatives to meet strategy and vision. Establish a timeline for them to become mission and revenue positive

Subsidize - programs provide a significant mission-related purpose and are incapable of producing enough revenue to support activity

The Master Budget

The budget is not a single document, rather, the master budget consists of several budgets that summarize all planned activities for the year. The master budget consists of:

Operational Budget

- Service/Product Revenue Forecast
- Operating Expense Budget
  - ➤ Direct program expenses
  - ➤ fixed expenses
- Fundraising Budget
- Budgeted Statement of Financial Activities

Financial Budget

- Cash Flow Projection Budget
- Debt Service Budget
- Investment Budget
  - ➤ Capital Budget
  - ➤ Reserve Budget
- Budgeted Statement of Financial Position

1. Service/ Product Revenue Forecast Budget

What is your market share? Begin by making assumptions as to the number of clients each program and service will serve. Review historical data - look at 3-year trends to determine client growth or decline. Look at the community of potential clients. Are there more or less potential clients in need of your services? How about competition? You can then use your data to estimate your market share going forward.

- Analyze revenue trend during that same 3-year window. What percentage increase or decrease – or rate of change is present?
- Establish the rate you will charge for each service or program. (* Fees collected from all revenue programs must cover all program expenses plus organizational fixed expenses.)
- You should end up with a document outlining your general assumptions for:
  - ➢ Potential number of clients for each service and program
  - ➢ Expected rate you will charge per client per program or service
  - ➢ Expected client revenue per program or service
  - ➢ Expected source of revenue (fees, restricted funds, contracts, operating reserve, etc.)

2. Operating Expense Budget

A. Determine Direct Costs for each program or service.

Examples of direct costs include:

- Salaries and benefits for staff members working exclusively on the program
- Travel expenses and equipment costs attributable to only the staff members who work on the program
- Supplies and materials for the program
- Vendor or contractor fees for the program

[In-kind contributions of goods or services should be budgeted at Fair Market Value (FMC). In-kind contributions will not impact your bottom line but still must be recorded and reported on your IRS 990 form. In addition, you will have a complete picture of actual total cost of each program to the organization.]

B. Determine Organization-wide Fixed or Shared Expenses

Examples of Fixed Expenses include:

- Any expenses that are not directly connected to a specific program and, have not been identified as a direct cost
- Administration and management expenses salaries and benefits (*See next slide for note
- Infrastructure costs), rent, utilities, equipment depreciation, software licenses
- Any costs that are incurred for the benefit of all the programs within the organization such as accounting, marketing costs, advocacy expenses, public relations, board of directors meetings

[* Note: Administration and Management fixed expenses. Non-program, nonprofit executives such as the executive director should define how their time is spent in percentage form. For example, if the executive director spends 40% time on program 1 and 25%time on program 2, only 35% of the executive director's salary and benefits should be attributed to administration and management. This is important because higher administration fixed expenses translate into higher reported overhead expenses. In other words, to outsiders (potential donors) the nonprofit looks as if it is less efficient than it really is. Be sure to include the percentage portion of executive time spent on a specific program in that program's budget.]

To determine the organization's overall expenses for the next 12 months, add the total direct expense budget for all programs, including fundraising, to the fixed expense budget. The resulting figure represents your total financial exposure for the next budget year.

3. Fundraising Budget

Before developing the fundraising budget, it would be helpful to know the current cost to raise a dollar (CRD). To determine your CRD divide total contributed revenue by total fundraising expenses.

$$\text{CRD} = \frac{\text{total contributed revenue}}{\text{total fundraising expenses}}$$

The lower the CRD, the more efficient you are at fundraising. A general rule of thumb for an acceptable CRD is 35% or less.

Fundraising budget should include:

- Program name (if it supports another program or service)
- Fundraising expenses associated with program
- Fundraising revenue associated with program including breakout of contributors and events
- CRD for program

4. The Budgeted Statement of Financial Activities

This statement contains all of the line items found in the regular Statement of Financial Activities, except it is a projection of what the Statement of Financial Activities will look like during the next fiscal year.

Statement of Financial Activities – compares program revenue against expenses for a specific point in time –month, quarter, etc.

The net assets section of this statement is where you will record the aggregate of

- Unrestricted donor contributions
- Unrestricted contribution revenue

- Net assets released from restrictions
- In-kind donations or services
- Unrealized investment income

5. Cash Flow Projection Budget

A cash flow projection budget will afford you the time it needs to plan for cash deficits and surpluses – allowing you to avoid a crisis situation. Knowing when key expenses and revenues are expected allows for better organizational decision making and increases your ability to deliver high-quality services and programs.

The components of your cash flow budget include:

- Payables – payroll and employee benefits, debt service, and any taxes
- Receipts- membership dues, program fees, donations, grants and contracts, event revenue, investment income

When preparing a cash flow projection budget you should first review your collections and payment policies. How quickly do you pay your bills? How long do you wait for revenue deposits? Your goal should be to collect receipts and make payables within 30 days of the transaction.

With your cash flow budget, make sure you break down each operational budget line item as to when and how much you expect to receive and spend over the next twelve months. (You can get this information from the Service Revenue Forecast and Operating Budgets.) Month-by-month, as well as quarterly planning, is best. If this is the first time you are creating a cash flow budget you can begin by reviewing your Statement of Cash Flow to give some insight on where cash came from and where it went. Next, break out the last quarter's expenses and revenues by line item and month. Use the resulting template to project forward cash flow.

6. Debt Service Budget

The debt service budget ties in directly with the cash flow budget as all debt payments will be in the form of cash. List all debt obligations by name, by fund responsible for payment, and by quarter.

7. Investment Budget

Many times, the nonprofit leadership believes that nonprofits' cannot make a profit or keep a profit (surplus). The truth is, nonprofits need working capital in order to continue delivering the mission that established the nonprofit. Without a profit, the longevity of the nonprofit would be in jeopardy. The only legal requirement concerning a nonprofit surplus is that it must be reinvested in the organization and its mission. Reinvest is what you should do. We have already mentioned the establishment of an operating reserve and capital fund accounts using program profits (surplus). If the nonprofit does not have an investment fund, its time to create a strategy to establish one showing notes due at beginning of quarter and those due at the end of the quarter.

The first thing your board will need to do is develop an investment policy defining the rules that govern investments. Consult with a local, but reputable, investment firm to establish an investment philosophy and fund objectives. Keep these three goals in mind when establishing a fund:

1. Liquidity – ability to get funds quickly
2. Reasonable rate of return on investments
3. Minimum risks to principal

Once you have a board approved investment policy, begin budgeting for surplus. Consumer-paid programs, such as membership fees and ticketed events, should generate profits. Assess all of your programs to determine their profitability potential.

8. Operating Reserve Fund

All nonprofits' need a reserve fund to deal with unexpected financial emergencies. Examples include:

- An unexpected use of cash
- An unexpected shortfall in revenue
- Downturn in local or regional economic environment
- Normal day-to-day changes in revenue and expenses

Developing and maintaining a reserve fund is also necessary if you accept government contracts and grants as many times they reimburse funds after you have made cash payments. The reserve fund insures financial stability and allows adequate cash flow on a day-by-day basis. Without a reserve budget, you risk the total collapse of the nonprofit.

The key to knowing how much to set aside for emergency use is understanding the nonprofits environment and risks. Management would be wise to perform some risk scenarios to calculate the odds and impact specific revenue reducing episodes would have on the nonprofit. Based on those probabilities, the board and management can establish a realistic reserve fund policy.

As much as possible, you must build some surplus, or profit, into your operating budget to build an appropriate reserve account. This can be achieved through unrestricted donations and/or slight rate increases in products/services sold through the nonprofit. Example: membership fees, journal subscriptions.

[Note – A general rule of thumb is for a nonprofit to set aside a minimum of 25% of the amount equal to the annual budget. That amount would allow three months of core operations should all revenue suddenly dry up. Many experts recommend 50 to 100% of the annual budget. But there is no one size fits all. Rules of thumb are not directives, just good advice. Nevertheless, the larger your reserve budget in relation to your operating budget, the greater flexibility you will have in responding to new opportunities that will drive your nonprofit toward the future your envision.]

9. Capital Budget

A capital budget helps you determine out how much money you need to purchase new equipment or to launch a new service. A capital budget includes asset purchases such as:

- Equipment
- Facility acquisition and improvements
- And sometimes, financial stability instrument like an operating budget reserve
- Depreciation

Capital budgets usually require a funding source separate from the operating budget. This funding is most commonly created through the use of unrestricted funds; a capital campaign for big ticket items such as a building.

10. Budgeted Statement of Financial Position

The Budgeted Statement of Financial Position contains all of the line items found in the regular Statement of Financial Position, except it is a projection of what the nonprofit's financial position will look like during the next fiscal year.

Statement of Financial Position – snapshot of organizational financial health (assets & liabilities) at a fixed point in time.

Some items to be recorded on this statement are:

- Aggregate of unrestricted donations
- Temporarily restricted funds
- Permanently restricted funds
- Capital campaigns
- Long term debt

Steps in Preparing the Master Budget

1.   Begin by merging the Service Revenue Forecast, Operating Expense, and Fundraising Budgets into one document (with four quarterly sections) to form your Operational Budget. Create your Budgeted Statement of Financial Activities. (Provides you will a snapshot of your overall financial picture going forward.)

2. After the Operating Budget has been prepared, develop the Financial Budget. The Financial Budget will show you the effects that the operating budget has on cash flow. To create the Financial Budget, merge the Cash Flow Projection, Debt Service, and Investment Budgets into one document. Create your Budgeted Statement of Financial Position.

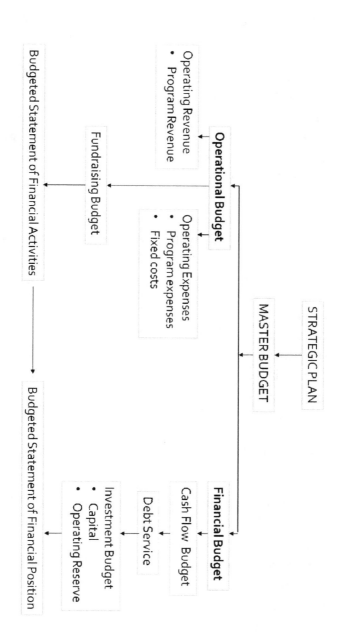

Congratulations! You have now created a rigorous, ongoing process for formulating the budget you need to close the mission gaps between your reality and your vision for the future. You are on your way to fully integrate strategy development with the financial planning process. Complete the budget process by creating a budget committee. (No more than 7 staff members. Rotate committee members annually giving all staff an opportunity to participate.) While all staff must be held accountable for mission delivery, it is wise to charge program managers with the responsibility of meeting with a budget committee monthly to review current data. Sharing up-to-date program information (as well as questions and concerns) improves organizational decision-making, eliminates financial surprises, and keeps the nonprofit focused on the mission.

Make Choices

Recognize the organization cannot pursue every idea, no matter how noble. The budget focus must be on the strategic goals that propel your organization into the future. Budgeting gives you one more opportunity to evaluate your program options against mission, strategy, and future vision.

Throughout the budgeting process continue to ask and answer:

- Which of our programs do we do really well? Build on your strengths.
- Which current program is essential to the client community and must be funded during your transformation into the future?
- Which new programs must be funded in order to carry the organization into the future?

The budget is the tool you use to eliminate non-essential programs; those programs that do not meet priority goals and objectives. This is important for several reasons:

a. Without a budget built around the vision priority, staff confusion as to what is important and what is not becomes an issue and ultimately allows employees to choose a priority. There can be no individual choices when it comes to organizational strategy priority. All units and employees must work on the same organizational priority if the organization is to achieve success.

b. Lack of vision budgeting means using resources on activities that are not a priority, making organizational success more difficult, or even impossible to achieve.

Remember, the annual budget plan dictates what the organization will do over the next 12 months. To align your budget with your strategic plan you must:

a. Build an annual budget showing what strategic plan activities the organization will engage in during the next 12 months.

b. Establish unit and departmental budgets to coincide with the unit strategies - those that meet organizational goals, objectives, and priorities.

c. Focus on the vision priority addressed in the strategic plan. Before you allocate resources in your budget, be certain to have those discussions with staff about how strategic plan goals and objectives will be integrated into operations and future programming.

d. Build measurable results (departmental, unit, organizational) into your budget plan to ensure the regular monitoring of progress toward achieving the vision.

e. Create a STOP sign metric for each program. If a program fails to achieve its intended results over a defined time period, for example, three months sequentially, suspend the program. Don't waste resources on a failed project. When suspending a program you give the organization time to re-examine, re-define, eliminate the program, or redirect expenses to another priority. No need to wait until the end of the budget year to discover a failed program.

More Closing Thoughts

1. The strategic plan, not the budget, must define *"what are"* the future nonprofit plans. The budget directs *"how resources"* needed to implement the strategy will be utilized.

2. Set a reasonable limit on the number of priorities that are both essential and fundable.

3. Engaging your front line staff in the budget process will give them the confidence to manage costs on a day-by-day basis as opposed to waiting for the traditional annual budget process to begin decision-making.

4. The budget must allow you to allocate money where it is needed (strategic priorities) when it is needed. The world is constantly changing. Your budget needs to be flexible enough to deal with the unexpected.

5. The budget must allow employees to track program progress and update assumptions as they occur. Don't be afraid to suspend a program that is failing miserably. Shift those resources to other programs or to financial budget needs. Resource allocation has to be synchronized across the nonprofit yet it cannot be a once-a-year occurrence.

6. Don't be afraid of using a rolling budget. At first, it may seem like a time consuming effort but once you get the

hang of it you will have an ever evolving revenue/cost driven based forecast rather than an immobile budget document that locks you into a prescribed and unchangeable path. The beauty of the rolling budget is it creates a culture where employees learn to evaluate program performance in real time, and thus, make better decisions. The rolling budget requires monthly updates to forecasts with actuals, and then a quarterly reforecast of a new 12-month rolling budget. Staying on top of the numbers on a monthly basis eliminates the multiple and stressful end of the budget year mad rush to collect and analyze performance and financial data. Implementing a rolling budget makes collecting and analyzing performance and financial data a regular part of employees' day-to-day routine.

Chapter Summary - Budget Plan

The budget plan dictates what the organization will do over the next 12 months to move the organization closer to the anticipated future and mission accomplishment.

- The <u>budget</u> is a blueprint showing what activities the organization, the unit, the department, and the employee will engage in during the next 12 to 18 months
  - ✓ It guides everyday operational decisions made by all employees.
  - ✓ It is flexible and adjusts to changing conditions
  - ✓ It is both an estimate of future revenue/expense and a benchmark to measure program financial effectiveness during the budget year
- The <u>budget</u> establishes organizational, unit, departmental, and employee objectives, expectations, and resource allocations
  - ✓ Everyone is responsible for meeting goals
  - ✓ It allows development of financial forecasting models

- It connects all work and programs to revenue and expense

Some Helpful Financial Ratios to Consider

Ratio	Ratio Equation	Ratio Target	Your Ratio
Debt Ratio	Total Debt/Total Assets	1 or less	
Current Ratio	Current Assets/Current Liabilities (Measures your ability to meet liability obligations during the current year)	1 to 1.9 Under 1 is too low Over 2 is too high	
Savings Ratio	Revenue – Expense/Total Expense (Shows how well you set aside money for future opportunities)	Ratio greater than 1 shows increase in savings	
Cash Ratio	Step 1 Annual Expense Budget/365 = One Day Cash Usage Step 2 Cash+Investments/One Day Cash Usage	180 days or higher Less than 90 days is too low	
Program Expense Ratio	Program Expense/Total Expense	65% or higher Under 65 is too low	
Average Collection Period	Days in the period X Average accounts receivable / Total amount of revenue in period (Indicates the amount of time clients are taking to pay their bills)	Under 30 days	
Average Days Payable	Days in the period X Average accounts payable / Total amount of purchases (Measures the average number of days you are taking to pay suppliers)	Under 30 days	
Program Profit Margin	Program profit/program revenue = % (For every dollar earned, shows % of profit)		
Interest Coverage	Operating profit/annual interest charged = % (Shows your ability to make loan payments, and/or ability to take on new debt)	Higher is better with 1 being too low	

Donors

Many nonprofits are funded by donors, grants, and foundations who are not the client community that benefits from the services provided by the nonprofit. This paradox between fund payers and receivers of service can challenge the nonprofit's thinking on loyalty. It shouldn't. The nonprofit's first priority must be the client community and the mission of the organization. Funders of the organization are important but they are not the reason why the nonprofit exists – the client community is the reason. Balancing the interests of funders with the needs of the client community can be tricky business. But it can be done if you know how to use storytelling as a way to engage your community.

Attracting donors and building relationships at all levels begins with your organization's unique story and vision for the future. But first, let's understand that all donors want to know what kind of impact the nonprofit has on solving the mission problem. Did you place 1,000 inner city kids living in poverty in a morning before-school daycare facility that provided a healthy breakfast? Although that is a good and worthy thing, potential donors may ask, "So what?" Other than doing a nice thing for humanity, how is your nonprofit different from others? How are the kids you treated doing in school compared to other children who did not receive your services? If your organization has been around for a long time, how many of your children graduated from high school? College? How does the health record of those served compare to those without the program? There are approximately 1.6 million nonprofits in the United States. Each one is competing for donors to support their cause. Americans are very generous giving over $300 billion to nonprofit organizations during 2013. That is a sizeable amount of money and if evenly divided among the nonprofit world it would equal $187,500 per nonprofit. But it does not work that way. People give to organizations that connect with their interests – not yours. So even if the nonprofit that feeds children before breakfast is a worthy cause to you, it may not be so worthy to a farmer with no children and a love for horses. In other words, your nonprofit is not going to get an even slice of the donation pie. It might get more, it might get less – it all depends on how well you tell your success story. There is a correct way to tell your organizations' story.

To begin, the story is not about your organization; the story is about one person who has benefited from your services. A few years back, Deborah A. Small of the University of Pennsylvania did some research on charitable giving.[4] She found that people give to causes that are attached to an identifiable individual in need and ignore other unknown groups of people in the same situation. One identifiable individual creates sympathy on the part of the donor; sympathy diminishes when donors are presented statistics for an unseen group of individuals with the same plight. Don't jump to the wrong conclusion that statistics and program outcomes are not important because they are. What the research is telling us is

[4] "Sympathy and callousness: The impact of deliberative thought on donations to identifiable and statistical victims." Deborah A. Small. *Science Direct*. March 3, 2006.

we need to tell the story – incorporating statistics - of one client of the nonprofit services who has documented successes.

Create Story Ambassadors

Choose several ambassadors of you most successful client's – individuals who have made the most of the nonprofit's services or programs. Plan and develop a two-minute YouTube video starring one client. Tell their story – where they come from, what obstacles they faced, what service they received and how these services have had a positive impact on their life. You want the story to evoke strong emotions on the viewer's part. Post you best ambassador on YouTube and on the home page of your web page for all visitors to see. (YouTube provides a link code to embed the video on your website.) Except for the home and about us tabs, keep everything else off of the home page while making the YouTube video as large as possible. The goal is to entice as many viewers as possible. Don't forget to link the ambassador with Facebook, Twitter, and blogs used by the nonprofit.

Make secondary YouTube ambassador videos for each program or service you offer and post those videos on the program page of each service or program.

Figure 29 Tips for Creating Client Story

1. Know your target audience. Who do you want to reach?
2. Think like a movie writer/director – develop a simple story line with an introduction, struggle, breaking point, solution, call-to-action. Make the story emotional, you want to tug on the heartstrings of the reader/viewer. You want them to react.
3. Connect the dots between your organization's work and its impact on your client community. Engage your

audience, you want them to see and feel the positive impact of the nonprofit.

4. Help the person who owns the story with a few simple targeted questions like:
    a. Before participating in our services what was your typical day like?
    b. At that time, what was your outlook on life?
    c. What is a typical day like now?
    d. What is your outlook for the future?
    e. What would you say to our donors if you met them?

5. For printed stories, add pictures that complement the story

6. Include "Donate Now" button at end of story

7. After "Donate Now" button insert a "More Information" button linking viewers to a one-page fact sheet which highlights nonprofits impact on society. This is for those viewers who want to know more before they donate.

8. Create a new story each month.

Figure 17. Example Client Story for Unsolicited Visitors to Web

 There are families like the Jones who struggle to make ends meet. Between the mother and father and a total of five part-time jobs, they could not make ends meet. After the winter Holiday season ended, Mr. Jones lost one of his part-time jobs they were evicted from their apartment on a cold night in January. They spent the rest of the winter living in their 1987 Chrysler wagon. (Click here for a two-minute video to see the Jones Family now.)

How could this happen you ask? They had their first children, (twins a boy with Downs Syndrome and a healthy girl) when they were just 16 years old. They both dropped out of high school and began taking on odd jobs – any kind of work they could find. They worked hard but with a limited education and a child with special needs, the world closed in on them. When their children started school, the Jones were referred to us.

Downtrodden and hopeless, they accepted our help. We found them an apartment and a permanent full-time job for Mr. Jones with health benefits for his family.

Because of you, and people like you, the Jones family now has hope for a better future. Because of you, they dream that one day they may be able to pay-it-forward.

| Donate Now |

Click here for more stories like the Jones'

Create a Donor Avatar

Follow the same process used earlier to create the client avatar to develop a donor avatar (Figure 34). Again, you will have several different avatars; high-level donors; nickel & dime donors; special event donors; annual giving; corporate; planned giving; government; and foundation grants. It is important that you understand each level of donors. Their passions and motives will be different. Each donor level will require a different fundraising approach tailored specifically to each levels emotional buttons.

Create Donor Ambassadors

Using the storytelling process, select strong donor supporters at each level to serve as ambassadors for the nonprofit. You should end with ambassadors of high worth individuals, annual givers, and even the $5 dollar a year donor. The goal is to have an ambassador for each giving group as you are trying to show "people like you" who support the nonprofit.

Thank Donors

Thank your donors using the same strategy that created the donation, with a story. Develop one minute YouTube videos thanking the donor for their help. Select someone from the client community who has benefited from the service or program funded by the donor. Produce a short, but sincere, thank you with the client telling why the donation mattered to him/her. Besides being the polite thing to do, a sincere thank you will resonate with the donor for several months and increase the odds that they will give again in the future.

Figure 31 Sample Donor Avatar

Mary Sue
Age 50

Avatar Profile

~Individual, but married with two adult children ~gives $1,872 year ~ age 50~ annual income of $77,500 ~ gives more near end of year holiday's ~ lives in suburbs ~ has college degree ~ Likes domestic travel ~ volunteers at local food pantry ~ dislikes marketing calls ~ has relative who was addicted to prescription drugs ~ Is frustrated by governments' lack of interest with help middle class Americans ~ Biggest fear is death to one of her from addict driving a car ~Wants to help you to

Figure 32 Sample Donor Ambassador Story

For John Q. Success, helping those less fortunate has always been a part of his life. John is a Harvard educated and a very successful businessman. He credits his parents for his success. Unlike John, his parents struggled to make ends meet. His father, George, graduated the eighth grade and immediately got a good job as a toolmaker. He married Joy, a book keeper at a small carpet manufacture, at eighteen; John was born the following year. They were a happy family and all was good until the Depression hit in 1928. Joy lost her job and George was reduced to part-time work. They lost everything. For the next 18 months, John and his parents lived in cardboard boxes, under bridges, in abandoned buildings, anywhere that provided a thin layer of shelter. They stood in food lines and ate at rescue missions. John's parents remained strong and kept hope alive. Then one day George found ABC Nonprofit. They found George a job and that changed everything for the family. John still remembers those days of log ago. He remembers his father always telling him to study hard, to work hard and to never forget that bad things can happen to good people. And never ignore the plight of others.

Please join me in making the world a better place.

> **Donate Now**

Click here for more donor ambassador stories.

Donor Milestones

As a nonprofit, data collection on your donors is as important as the data you collect on the client community. Fortunately, social media can assist you in this area. If you collect no other data on your donors, capture their email address, Facebook, and LinkedIn profiles, and Twitter name. Facebook and LinkedIn can provide you with donor birthdays, work anniversaries, and other important milestones in the donors' life. You want to know about these milestones so that you can email, Facebook, or Tweet best wishes. Use every opportunity available to remind your donor that you still exist. For milestone messages, create a Vine or Instagram video (5 seconds) wishing the donor happiness on their milestone. No asking for money, no client success story, just a small group of clients reciting a scripted best wishes message. Videos can be tweeted, emailed, or posted to Facebook. Remember, a posting on Facebook or Twitter will be seen by all of the donors' friends and family giving you free exposure to others who might not know of your existence. Be sure to capture the profiles of the donors' Facebook and Twitter friends in order to cultivate them as future donors. Start by sending them video congratulations on their milestones posted to social media. Do not ask for money, you just want exposure. Your development team will want to add these names to potential future marketing/fundraising campaigns. (By the way, these same strategies work for members of a membership organization.) You will need to be careful not to overdo it with donor social media friends. Pursue only those social media friends that post a positive response to one of your milestone videos.

Donor Engagement

Successful fundraising begins and ends with donor engagement. All of the strategies discussed before are about creating opportunities to connect emotionally with donors.

Donors will continually give to causes they care about only if that organization cares about the donor. Keep your donors engaged with the nonprofit. Email them monthly updates and success stories. (Always provide an unsubscribe option, on emails. Some donors may not wish to receive monthly updates.) Keep the update short, something that can be read in 10 to 20 seconds. Graphs, simple charts, and visuals are easiest to read. A short video (15 seconds) could replace text. Post updates on the website as well. Always remember, donors usually give to more than one nonprofit – your goal is to make your nonprofit the donors' favorite.

Consider creating an organizational blog on your web page, if you don't have one, and invite donors to be your writers. Topics can be simple – why do I care about this nonprofit? How this nonprofit makes an impact on the world? Etc. Involving your donors with blogging keeps your donors connected with the nonprofit while at the same time providing valuable content to be shared with your stakeholders.

By no means do these strategies constitute a complete listing of donor engagement activities. It is not meant to be. The main takeaway here is to create a culture whereby the nonprofit continually thinks of the donors as partners and finds ways to connect them with the client community; finds ways to keep them engaged with the work of the nonprofit. Do this well and you will have the resources to deliver outstanding services to your client community well into the future.

Chapter Summary

There are different types of donors. There are high-wealth, one-time givers, special event givers, regularly scheduled givers, and nickel and dime givers just to name a few. If you want their money you must find ways to actively engage them with the nonprofit. Create donor avatars for each major type of giving to help you understand what they like and dislike. Use story ambassadors to promote the nonprofit to potential givers. Good donors will find you, new donors. And of all things, never forget to thank your donors regardless of how small the gift may be.

MAJOR TAKEAWAYS FROM BOOK

Over the past decade or two, research has taught us that successful organizations engage all employees in the management of the enterprise. Top down decisions seldom bring positive returns. Rather, it is the routine and continuous contributions of the non-executive employee that brings organizational success.

Takeaway 1. Managers should make it a routine practice to talk about why the organization exists, what it stands for, how it conducts business, and who it serves. The more employees understand the organization's unique situation the better they will be able to help the organization prosper and grow.

Takeaway 2. Train all employees in the fundamentals of organizational finance. Nonexecutive employees make decisions every day – decisions that impact organizational finances. Employees who understand how the organization designates direct vs indirect costs will be better able to manage both types of costs in their department. Employees who can read and understand the organization's Statements of Financial Position, Financial Activities, and Cash Flow will make better decisions now as well as be better prepared to make forecast models of future organizational spending and revenue.

Takeaway 3. Managers should make it a routine practice to talk about the challenges and trends confronting the organization's client community. What is the big problem facing the client community? What keeps them awake at night? What is the organization doing to help the client community solve the big problem?

Takeaway 4. Connect all employee work with the mission. Seems like an obvious observation but you might be surprised to learn just how disconnected many employees are to the mission. A 2013 Gallop Poll found that: only 29% of American workers are actively engaged in their work; 54% are not engaged (lack motivation, not invested in organizational outcomes); and 18% are actively not engaged (unproductive, spread negativity). While we would like to believe that this is not the case in the nonprofit world we cannot assume the statistics are any different for this class of worker and must address employee connectivity head-on.

Takeaway 5. Expect every employee to be a leader. Build a culture where information is shared throughout the organization. Hoarding information leads to silo's and can prevent employees in other departments from making the right decisions for the organizational. Include non - executive employees from all levels in management, communication, and strategy meetings. Encourage employees to communicate with each other, especially those in other departments, and to share insights they have gained from experience and training.

Takeaway 6. Make tough decisions. Deliver only those programs that are highly mission related or produce positive revenue. Eliminate programs that are marginally related to the mission, especially if they break even or lose revenue. (If a marginal program breaks even it still uses resources that could be allocated to a highly rated mission program.) Reducing programs will reduce expenses and increase focus on priority mission services.

Takeaway 7. Watch out for mission creep. Many nonprofits lose focus of the mission and how it should be delivered. Mission creep has a way of pushing and pulling an organization into too many directions, weakening the organization's capabilities to deliver on its stated mission. Unless you are vigilant in addressing top mission priorities, mission creep will slowly take over and divert valuable resources to ideas that **don't meet strategic priorities.**

Takeaway 8. Focus first on the longer-term strategic aspirations. Board directors often prefer to spend most of their time on the current challenges. It is easy, it is comfortable to stay in the present and address current issues. However, strategic thinking requires board directors to abandon the rear view mirror philosophy and to look forward. Staff is paid to handle today's emergency while the board plans for tomorrow. Unless today's problem is catastrophic in nature, board intervention in normal operational aches often ends up creating a new set of problems.

Takeaway 9. Be disciplined about choosing a strategic future. Be careful to avoid basing your future on unconfirmed assumptions or hunches. You will make better choices when you carefully weigh proposed strategy against your mission, people, core competencies, and assets.

Takeaway 10. Recognize new strategies usually require mindset shifts. Think of the nonprofit organizations as a living organism. It consists of human beings, who have hopes, fears, beliefs, and emotions. And change is predictable in that it evokes unpleasant and unjustifiable thoughts and emotions. Don't ignore the predictable and groundless reactions that will accompany new strategy development as it can undermine the whole process? Your approach should be to anticipate and identify those with less than positive mindsets and engage them early and often and convert them into believers in a better future.

Takeaway 11. Establish metrics that measure short- and long-term success of the strategy. Do not roll out a new strategy or program without performance metrics. Some of your existing metrics may still work with new programs, but it is likely that you one or two new metrics. Focus on how the strategy or program is meeting short and long-term targets.

Takeaway 12. Be vigilant about recruiting board directors who possess the skill sets needed to carry the organization forward. Occupational, geographic, gender, religious, and racial diversity is necessary for a healthy board. More perspectives on organizational issues will lead to better strategy and solutions.

Takeaway 13. Help your donors and clients tell their stories to the community at large. Building a reputation as a positive force in the community will bring the nonprofit new ideas, new growth, and new money.

CPSIA information can be obtained
at www.ICGtesting.com
Printed in the USA
BVHW070228131218
535503BV00018B/414/P